UPHILL ALL THE WAY

UPHILL
ALL THE WAY

A Miner's Struggle

by
LORD TAYLOR OF MANSFIELD

SIDGWICK & JACKSON
LONDON

ISBN 0 283 97911 9

Printed in Great Britain at
the St Ann's Press, Park Road, Altrincham, Cheshire WA14 5QQ
for Sidgwick and Jackson Limited
1 Tavistock Chambers, Bloomsbury Way,
London WC1A 2SG

477

To Clara and Bernard, my wife and son. And to the British Coal Miners, especially those in the Nottinghamshire and Derbyshire area.

Acknowledgements

I would like to express my very real gratitude to Lady Llewelyn-Davies, Mr and Mrs G. R. Hovington, and Mr D. R. W. Greenslade for their invaluable help in editing and typing the manuscript, and obtaining many of the photographs.

Contents

Illustrations

Foreword

by Rt Hon. Harold Wilson, O.B.E., F.R.S., M.P.

I believe that many of those who will read Bernard Taylor's *Uphill All the Way* will judge it to be one of the best social and industrial records of this century. It portrays, in a moving personal style, a part of our society which has given so much to the whole of our society, an age which has largely passed, but which has bequeathed its memories, its scars, and its ideals to a new generation.

It is the story, first, of a part-rural, part-mining community, in the 1890s and the early years of this century, low wages and a struggle to live. The role of the Methodist church, dominant in the community, but also the alma mater of a young pit-lad where he first learns as an embryo local preacher to express himself in public. It is there that he senses the revelations and dreams which later, under the pressure of social problems and the brutality of industrial confrontation, become more clearly directed towards changing society, through local and national politics.

And, above all, loyalty to the Union. From his first day as a frightened pit-boy in the darkness to his election as a check-weighman, Bernard Taylor's life was the pit and the mining community. He records the impact of the 1921 stoppage when the miners, on their own not for the last time, took on the coal owners in that premature post-war orgy of de-control of the mines. We read what it means for the family, for the village. We read a moving account of the pit-ponies, brought to the surface, and gambolling about the fields in their freedom.

Central to the book, and to the author's own life, is 1926. By this time a local union official, he plays his part in providing relief for the families affected, and, by organizing meetings, with visiting speakers such as Aneurin Bevan, maintaining the morale of his work-mates. And then the collapse of the resistance, and the brutal reaction of the coal-masters. The official union was no longer recognized; in its place was the hated breakaway Spencer Union. Bernard Taylor tells of the obscene reaction of the colliery management when he sought his job back. He had been loyal to the union. His application was met by management turning its back, lifting up its coat-tails—'speak to my bottom.'

For twelve years he was in the wilderness—a collector, outside colliery land, of trade union subscriptions for the un-recognized official union; a twelve-year record of arrogant victimization.

Trade union history in the late thirties surrounded the issue of the Spencer Union, and the great Harworth colliery dispute of 1937. Bernard Taylor was accredited by the union as their liaison officer to Harworth. Backed by the Mineworkers Federation of Great Britain, and the T.U.C., they won their battle; after riots, arrests and Stafford Cripps appearing, and refusing payment, for the defence. And, victory achieved, Bernard Taylor was welcomed by management to his old job. His personal account is part of the history of the British trade union movement; what we have in this book is history as seen by one of the principal participants.

But this is a record not only of trade union history. It is a record of local government, by a local councillor, a council chairman; it is inspired by the record of battles in the field of health, and mental health, and human stories of what an effete law of workmen's compensation meant for the casualties of the mining industry.

The coal industry in war-time, the coal industry in post-war reconstruction. The author, now an M.P. fighting in the House of Commons for the men who created him, the men for whom he spoke with a quiet and effective authority. Parliamentary Private Secretary to the Minister of National Insurance, he urged the issues for which he had fought those hopeful battles as trade union official and local government representative over the hard years. And national legislation in that post-war parliament reflected the struggle in the Mansfield Woodhouse council chamber and the Nottingham miners' union.

And then—a Minister of the Crown, in the department where those early, apparently unrealizable dreams could become a legislative and executive reality. Workmen's compensation, insurance, industrial disease—the pioneering of Mansfield Woodhouse in dealing with mental disability.

And finally, the Lords, where one Noble Lord—and he has friends and partners from backgrounds similar to his own—fights on for these issues, once local, which have now become national.

And the fight will go on, as long as the Jack Lawsons and the Bernard Taylors, the Bill Blytons and the Joe Slaters—and their House of Commons colleagues—are there to represent the anxieties and hopes, the fears and the dreams of the people who gave them voice.

Not for them the recognition of tired and cynical pressmen and the accolade of the other media. They are the voice of the England of the ages, the England of the industrial revolution. The England which will live when the spurious purveyors of grab and greed, of the speculative society, are gone and unmourned by the England which will survive, and survive enriched by the struggles of those commemorated in this book.

For it is a book to which academic researchers will turn and turn again. It is a book which will provide historical backing and inspiration for all of those who have to carry the torch of the Nottingham miners into the future. Above all, in an era when the Labour Party proudly embraces the sons of those from Nottingham, Scotland, Wales, and the North as their standard bearers, together with so many talented young candidates and M.P.s from very different backgrounds, this is a book which should be compulsory reading for all who aspire to represent Labour in the generation of the seventies, the eighties and beyond.

Reading this book, they will learn what the Labour movement is about. Not only they, but the wider Labour movement, political and trade union, will be enriched certainly by what they have read, but still more by what they have learnt, and, learning, have resolved to make part of their contribution to the Britain which the Labour movement was created to serve.

CHAPTER I

Birthplace and Parentage

I was born on 18 September 1895 at Mansfield Woodhouse in the county of Nottinghamshire. Then it was a rural village; today it is synonymous with industry and workers. Geographically, it is situated on the edge of what is left of the old Sherwood Forest. It first began, many centuries ago, as a tiny rustic farming settlement set in a glen of the great forest, which at one time covered 200 square miles of the country. The peasant people made a simple living from farming and home crafts, and made use of the abundant timber to provide their homes. This was before the arrival of the Romans who also settled here, as was proved by the discovery of two Roman villas some years ago.

For many decades the main industries were agriculture and stone quarrying. The foundations and the lower parts of the Houses of Parliament contain stone from the quarries of Mansfield Woodhouse. For many years before the invasion of coal-mining textiles were an important part of the industrial life of the village. The sinking of the two collieries, Sherwood in 1902 and Mansfield (locally known as Crown Farm) in 1905, brought great changes, but Mansfield Woodhouse has a history of which the present generation is proud.

Local historians have recorded many references to its antiquity many decades before the beginning of coal-mining operations. This, however, is not the place to enlarge further upon the geographical situation and antiquity of the place, or even the folklore of Robin Hood and his Merry Men.

The circumstances in which my parents met were unique, considering that they lived twenty miles apart. Unlike today when distance is no obstacle, a century ago twenty miles was a great distance: the only way to cover it was on foot, under your own steam.

My mother's home was in a remote part of Nottinghamshire, the village of Caunton near Newark and it is doubtful, apart from the circumstances which brought them together, whether they would have ever met. One thing they had in common: they came from agricultural stock. But their acquaintanceship opened in an unusual way. I have often heard the story and have been fascinated by it and amazed at the circumstances, and I relate it to indicate one of the methods used to obtain employment in agriculture a century ago.

In 1879 my father was hired at the October Fair in Mansfield market-place by a local farmer, as a waggoner. This was a term commonly used in agriculture, and designated the nature of the job: to look after and work with the horses on the land. At the same time my mother was hired in Newark market-place as a domestic farm servant. This was the way they were referred to nearly a century ago. At this time my father and mother were seventeen and fifteen years respectively. My mother, one year before, had lost her father—killed in an accident on a farm. This was a tragedy for the family: the breadwinner had gone; there was no Workmen's Compensation in those days, and the family was receiving Poor Law Relief from the Southwell Board of Guardians. There were seven children; the three elder, one of whom was my mother, were written off as old enough to work: the remaining four were allowed two shillings and sixpence a week each; my grandmother was told that there would be no allowance for her—she would have to go out to work.

This domestic experience was never forgotten by my mother. She often referred to it and remarked that one half of the people did not know how the other half lived. By nature she was a rebel and the circumstances of her early life fanned the flames of rebellion.

The hiring in 1879 was not my parents' first entry into employment. My father began work on the land at the age of eight. Attendance at school was voluntary, and the education of children in the 1860s was irregular, and many were unable to read and write.

In 1879, when the previous yearly contract had ended, and people were seeking pastures new, hiring was the method. The farmers and their wives would come annually to the hiring fairs and choose their servants; tell the applicants who they were, where the farm was situated, and the wage. When the bargain had been struck between the two parties, the custom was that the servants received what was described as the 'Fastening Penny'. This was a token that a contract had been entered into, and was legally binding.

On the agreed date my father and mother arrived separately at North Lodge Farm, Mansfield Woodhouse, complete strangers. Three years later, they married at Caunton Parish Church. The Reverend R. S. Hole, who was the Vicar and who later became the Dean of Rochester, officiated. My father often told me that when he was paying the fee, Mr Hole said to my mother, 'Here you are, Mary Ann! This is for you.' From the union there were four sons; I was the youngest.

The house in which I was born was a stone cottage, Number 4 in Rose Lane, Mansfield Woodhouse. It is still there, more than a hundred years old. The present owner, an old friend of mine, occupies the place. He has made a good job in renovation and in the provision of sanitary amenities which were non-existent at the time of my birth.

It was on 18 September that I was born—the last son. When I grew up I recall my mother saying to me (I really think in the form of a confession), 'My boy, at the time of your birth, you were an unwanted child.' In amazement I recall asking the question: 'Why, mother?' The reply was perfectly straightforward: it was a struggle to make ends meet with three, in spite of good domestic management ('pinching and scraping' as she called it) and another one to feed and clothe was not a pleasant prospect. My father's wage was eighteen shillings a week. Compared with today the value of money was very different, I know, but, taking this into account, it was a poor wage. Less than three shillings per person per day, including rent (which was either two shillings and sixpence or three shillings per week) meant spending wisely, scraping and sacrificing. Certainly there was no margin for luxuries. They did their best for us, but the diet—mostly bread and potatoes

3

—was more starch than protein. I recall that one of the hot meals often provided was 'Johnny Grundy' or 'Hot-Pot'. We had a name for it locally: 'Fifty-to-one': fifty pieces of potato to one piece of meat. To express our delight when we got a piece of meat, we would call 'Snap'.

My father, before my birth, had moved from North Lodge Farm and was now employed on Dovecote Farm, still in Mansfield Woodhouse. This was smaller in acreage. Here he was not only the horseman but also did all kinds of jobs common to mixed farming. The farm was tenanted by a Mr Thrutchley, an ardent Methodist. He had a grandson, and together they worked the farm with my father's help and there was a good relationship between them. When Mr Thrutchley gave up the tenancy, my father left agriculture.

He often took me as a small child to the farm, which was near home. Although so young, I still remember two magnificent horses, one weighing a ton, the other nineteen hundredweight. I thought they were wonderful to look at and admire. I think it was this experience that created in me a love and admiration of horses, and to this day they are my favourite animals.

I think I was four years old when my father left agriculture and went to work on the surface at Shirebrook Colliery, a local pit three miles from Mansfield Woodhouse. He remained there until his retirement in 1927. He was a good man, retiring, shy and reserved. His preoccupations were his work, gardening, and doing the best for his family. To me he was one of nature's gentlemen.

The last years of his life were not as rewarding as they should have been. After a lifetime of hard work, from the age of eight to sixty-five, he had two problems, one economic and one physical. He had only £200 to see him through the rest of his life, for he had a dread of applying for Poor Law Relief. On retirement his weekly income was ten shillings a week, until my mother also reached sixty-five and they had another ten shillings a week. Often I heard him say, 'If youth did know what old age did crave, they would never spend a penny they ought to save.' Also his health was poor. Each succeeding winter after his retirement he had a bad time with his lungs.

4

I have no doubt they were affected by dust from the pit. At that time silicosis had only just been recognised as an industrial disease and it was much more difficult to establish a claim for compensation than it is now. Doctors signed certificates for bronchitis, or emphysema, or both.

During the last winter of his life, when he was seventy-two, it was a struggle for my father to breathe, and eventually he thankfully passed into the unknown. In temperament and disposition my parents were so different, but they lived together happily for more than fifty years. Together they struggled. When they died, which was within a little over two years of each other, all their children were alive, and after cremation their ashes were mixed and the four of us scattered them under a sycamore tree, within a short distance of North Lodge Farm where, fifty-nine years before, they had first met.

CHAPTER II

At School

At the age of four or five, I began school. On reflection, I have often wondered how it was that I was not sent to the same school as my older brothers but I do not recall having enquired or having been told the reason. I can only assume—but I am sure the assumption is the valid explanation—that it happened as follows:

The only school in Mansfield Woodhouse up to 1900 was a denominational one (Church of England). It was built in 1845, and since then has always been known as the National School. It is still functioning, but then it was inadequate to provide for the growing increase in the school population. The newly formed County Councils in 1888 were assuming greater responsibilities in the county districts for education and other services. The authorities of the denominational schools held on to what they had but were unwilling, possibly for financial reasons, to cater for the phenomenal increase in the school population in Nottinghamshire, brought about by industrial development. Mansfield Woodhouse, where this was happening at the beginning of the twentieth century, was faced with such a situation. The Nottinghamshire County Council, as the local Education Authority, began to make additional educational provision for the increasing school population. In those days it was known as Elementary Education, and the form it took was the setting up of 'Board Schools', non-denominational and administered by the County Council. The whole expenditure was met out of public funds.

My parents were radical nonconformists, and, now there was alternative educational provision, I was sent to the Board School. This was new but the need was pressing. While the

6

new school was being built temporary premises had to be hired. Between 1899 and 1903 there was no real school as we know it now. A big house in Castle Street was made available and rented by the County Council. This was the Infants' School and it was here that my education began, either in 1899 or 1900. For the junior and senior scholars the old Baptist Chapel in Portland Street and the Primitive Methodist schoolroom were used. Meanwhile the new school was being built in Oxclose Lane. Knowing this was to be our new school we watched its progress, and, in 1903, it was opened.

All the scholars were transferred to this brand new school; we thought it marvellous, judging by the standards of those days. It was a fine building of three blocks : Infants, Girls and Boys. All the scholars thought it was wonderful : it had flushed toilets, heated water pipes in the class-rooms, and a playground, asphalt of course, but, alas, no playing-field with soft green grass. The playground was used for half an hour a day for the morning and afternoon breaks of a quarter of an hour each. If in the excitement you perchance fell down the result was grazed knees and hands. You hit the hard, solid surface with a bang; then it was tears and blood, and if it was the result of rough play, you sometimes received a reprimand and the cane, which was not forbidden in those days. Indeed I recall occasions when it was used quite liberally! I was now eight years of age, and this new building was to be my new educational home for the next five years.

Truancy or 'playing wag', as it was called, was a practice frequently exercised. The bogey man was the School Attendance Officer or the School Bobby. If he made a 'capture' during school hours, he would take the offender back to school, and, if the headmaster was satisfied it was a deliberate act of truancy, the pupil was punished. In later years as a member of the County Education Committee I found cases of truancy almost non-existent, and today it is very rare. I believe the reason for the truancies when I was at school was that the parents and grandparents of my generation had only just emerged into the system of compulsory education and attendance at a school, and the awareness of education had not taken root. How exhilarating and satisfying it is that for the past forty or fifty years the growth of awareness on the part of parents and children has taken place. Now if one sees a child in the street during school hours, one does not imagine that he is playing truant.

A new headmaster, Mr R. H. Bannister, was appointed to the new and first non-denominational Board School in Mansfield Woodhouse. I must make a reference to him. Of course there were times when, as scholars, we thought he was hard and exacting, but he was a good man and had the educational welfare of his pupils very much in his mind. For many years I have heard appreciation of his influence, and I have no doubt this would be the opinion of the generation of boys who attended Oxclose Lane school in those days of sixty-eight years ago. How fitting and nostalgic it is that in imagination you can still see the desk at which you sat, the black-board in the distance and the teacher with chalk in hand, endeavouring to impart knowledge to his or her pupils!

When I look at my biographical notes in *Who's Who* or *Dodd's Parliamentary Companion*, I find these words: 'Educated at Oxclose Lane Council School'. I am quite proud of this, and pleased to acknowledge my indebtedness. Of one thing, on reflection, I am sure: I was not a brilliant scholar, certainly not a high-flier, as a brilliant pupil is called now. The curriculum was restricted to the three Rs. I had my likes and dislikes even in this restricted field. At arithmetic I was just ordinary; at drawing hopeless. I preferred reading, composition and dictation and at these subjects I did not do badly.

In the classroom was a board upon which, every day, the number in the class was recorded. It was seldom less than sixty. This figure is an indication of the then urgent need to meet the statutory educational requirements in this area, where the population was expanding, and the fertility rate was high. The average size of families would be six, excluding parents.

Many friendships were formed among the scholars and some of them survived long after leaving school. Today it is a refreshing pleasure to meet and converse with those who were scholars at Oxclose Lane School, though their numbers get less as so many have passed away. There was a strong school patriotism, revealing itself in a keen rivalry between the new school and the old. The well-established National School had nicknames such as 'Nats' for the old school, and 'Bugs' for the new school scholars. Games like football and cricket were organized between the two schools. The rivalry and determination of both sides to win was amazing. There were other rivalries, and sometimes an exhibition of fisticuffs. In the winter there would be snow fights. The new school was referred to as the 'Chapel School', the National School as the 'Church School' and there was a distinct dividing line. Happily the gulf has long since disappeared, and today there is unity between the scholars of both schools.

Reflecting over the years, I feel a sense of gratitude to the school, the headmaster and the teaching staff, and especially to Miss Kimberley and Miss Greensmith, two fine ladies. They married two local gentlemen—Mr Reason and Mr Beeton and settled in Mansfield Woodhouse where they brought up their families. But they have now passed on.

At eleven years of age either ambition or curiosity or a mixture of both made me start my first job at the local hospital, cleaning the cutlery. There was no stainless steel at that time. To avoid rust, the cutlery had to be cleaned at least once a week. A piece of cloth, bath-brick and elbow grease were the tools of the trade. A few months of this and I became an errand boy at the local butcher's. (The business is still in the same family.) I had to go to the customers for the orders and deliver meat on Friday evenings and Saturdays. The baskets I had to carry were very heavy when full, and there was no bicycle or van as transport. It was much more pleasant returning to the shop than going on the outward journey, but it was interesting meeting people, and getting to know their likes and dislikes. It was a study in domestic economics to watch them work out how much they could afford; the cheapest cuts were much in demand. I learnt quite a lot about the carcasses of beef, pork and mutton, and also the ingredients of things like sausages, black-puddings and pork pies. I continued in this job for two years until I reached my thirteenth birthday, the school leaving age at that time.

I remember clearly that my thirteenth birthday, in 1908, was on a Friday. It appears strange to remember the day of this particular birthday when I have forgotten so many others. Maybe it was the last day of the school week and the fact that I was leaving and saying 'good-bye' to the school. An important decision had to be made and I was faced with the alternative of either staying at the butcher's and learning the trade, or seeking other employment. I am sure my parents would have preferred that I learned the trade of butcher, but my three elder brothers had gone to work at the pit, and, for good or ill, I chose to go to work on the surface at the colliery, thus beginning my full-time working life as a pitman.

CHAPTER III

Starting Work

This was an occasion, a red-letter day, an important milestone in life's journey, a new venture; the routine of the past years at school was ended, the prospect of going out into the world was not unattractive, and the opportunity of bringing a little grist to the domestic mill was welcomed.

It was at Pleasley Colliery in 1908, four miles from home, that I began work as a screen worker on the surface. This job involved picking the dirt and foreign matter from the coal as it moved along the belt: a tedious, monotonous, back-aching job. There was little, if anything, to inspire, but it was something, a beginning, and I cherished the hope that there were prospects of something different. I was aware that within twelve months I would be fourteen and it was then permissible to work underground.

1908 was a landmark for the miners of Britain, for it was in that year that a Bill was passed through Parliament restricting the hours of work underground to eight hours a day. This came into operation in 1909, and for a few months therefore I worked a nine-hour day from 6.30 a.m. to 3.30 p.m. The journey of four miles each way to and from the colliery was not included in the nine hours. The eight-mile journey to and from the pit in winter was by the paddy train, run by the Midland Railway Company. This train was made up of very old railway coaches, discarded passenger coaches that had bare wooden seats, no heating and no lighting. The journey was cold and cheerless. The cost was one and three-pence per week—or as we would say now in these decimilization days, seven new pence.

During the summer of 1909, with other men and boys I

walked the daily eight miles, the main reason being to save the train fare. It was forty-eight miles a week, and fifty-one hours of work. Saturday was worked only six hours.

They were long, tiring days. I rose in the morning at 4.45 a.m. and arrived home at 5.0 p.m. The wage I received was one shilling and threepence per day. When my first week's pay of seven shillings and sixpence was due, my mother said, and it was an instruction, 'Do not forget to see the Union Man and join the Miners' Federation!' It was not a closed shop in those days and the contribution for boys under sixteen was three pence per week. It was good advice, for which I have always been grateful; from 1908 till 1944 I was a member of the Miners' Federation of Great Britain, and from 1944 to 1966 a member of the National Union of Mineworkers. At the time of my retirement in 1966, I had been a member of the Miners' Union for fifty-eight years. I would very much have liked to have continued my membership by a token payment, but there was no provision for this in the rules and it is now only in spirit that I am a member. When one Union for Mineworkers was formed in 1944, succeeding the Miners' Federation, the conference of the miners who accepted the change and the new organizational structure, was held in my native county in the city of Nottingham. This event was the culmination of the dreams and propaganda of many miners throughout the British coal-field for many years.

On 18 September 1909 I was fourteen, and now eligible to work underground, a prospect I had been looking forward to for twelve months. I obtained a job at Langwith Colliery, but in spite of my high hopes this job only lasted a day. There were two pits in Mansfield Woodhouse much nearer home but a chum persuaded me to go to Langwith, five miles away. I still remember going down in the cage for the first time. The shaft was 1,500 to 1,600 feet in depth. The cage began to move and it was a new and queer experience. To my surprise and alarm when the ascending and descending cages passed in the middle of the shaft, I thought we were ascending. In a few moments I was soon disillusioned when we were landed safely at the pit bottom. It was certainly a relief to me and to the other twenty occupants that we had got over the initial experience. A common feeling of relief, and gratitude to the engine winder (as he was designated) was shared by all when we landed safely.

I was put to the job of joining the tubs to form a train, which were then taken by haulage rope to the coal face, a distance of anything between one and two miles. The pit name for this kind of job was called 'coupling-on'. Joined together, the tubs would be attached to the haulage rope by a clip and it was like a train or a set of waggons on the railway. They would move away into the darkness at a speed of three to four miles an hour. On arrival at their destination the clip would be detached from the rope by a boy who was designated a 'knocker-off'. At this point the tubs would be taken, drawn by a pony accompanied by a boy called a pony driver, to the men at the coal face to be filled with coal, a further distance of half a mile or more.

During that first day I was called into an office and told by the under-manager that I would have to work on the night shift. My feeling was that it would be a novelty. But when I arrived home after my first day underground and reported this to my mother, her reactions were very unfavourable. She said, 'No! That distance away! I should not sleep in my bed! The thought of locking the door and you away in the darkness and danger of the pit, I should be on the night shift too! You must try to get a job at a pit that doesn't work on nights!' There was no questioning her decision, so my stay at Langwith Colliery lasted one day. She would not allow me to fetch even the one day's pay. It was goodbye to Langwith Pit for ever.

Years afterwards, I recall addressing a group of National Coal Board officials and succumbed to the temptation of relating the Langwith Pit story. Among the audience was the deputy chairman of the East Midlands Divisional Coal Board, a Mr Glossop, who at one time after 1909 was the Manager of Langwith Colliery. The story amused him, and he said, 'We had better pay you with interest; but on second thoughts, you left without giving notice to terminate your contract so we had better call it a day.'

After the one-day episode at Langwith Pit, I obtained a job

at Sherwood Colliery, one of the two in Mansfield Wood-house. In those days of sixty-two years ago there were no training facilities. During the past twenty-five years an elaborate and greatly needed system of training for young entrants has been in operation, and it reflects great credit on the National Coal Board. In my youth, you were just pitched into it and you learned from experience. The usual practice was to put young boys going underground for the first time to the job of 'door trapping'. Everyone in mining knew the kind of job this was. Over the years it had grown and become a tradition. Proper and adequate ventilation in the pit is absolutely necessary for safety. Air is forced down the shaft at great velocity, and when it gets to the bottom it has to be directed throughout the whole of the workings in the pit. To achieve this, doors are made as airtight as possible; otherwise the air would go where it liked instead of where it was needed. The air in the pit at the bottom of the downcast shaft was very cold, but by the time it had reached the workings along circuitous routes, in some cases two miles from the shaft bottom, the temperature had considerably increased and could be described as hot, hence the reason why the men at the coal face wore little clothing. The job of the new boy, the door trapper, was to open the doors to allow the ponies hauling the tubs to and from the working places to pass through and then see they were closed. It was a simple operation but a very important one.

At this time there were 250 ponies in Sherwood pit. They were well housed and well fed, but it was an unnatural life for them. Since those days a technical and mechanical revolution has taken place, and now there are no ponies in the pit, and this change in the method of transport from the coal-face to the pit bottom, by electrically-driven conveyors instead of ponies, is general throughout the British coal-field.

The memory of sitting behind the door alone and most of the time in darkness still haunts me, in spite of the many years that have passed since 1909. You were isolated and the Davy Safety Lamp was easily extinguished; the door trapper's lamp had to be lent to the pony drivers, who were responsible for a constant supply of tubs to the men at the coal-face and whose wages depended on this operation—no output of coal, no wages. Until the lamp was relighted, the pony driver had the door trapper's lamp, and for most of the day this was happening; when one lamp had been relighted, another had gone out, and there you were alone, and afraid, in the darkness, listening to the timber roof supports cracking and making weird noises—and at fourteen years of age the mind is impressionable. Pit darkness has to be experienced to be believed. It reminds me of the Methodist lay preacher at the village chapel who took for his text, 'Darkness, gross darkness covered the face of the earth'. In explanation he said, 'Well, my friends, we all know what darkness is. Depending upon the season of the year, it comes early or late, but I am unable to give a satisfactory reason for gross darkness. After thinking about it, the only conclusion I can come to is that gross darkness is a hundred and forty-four times darker than dark.' This is as good a description of pit darkness as any I can think of.

My job of door trapping did not last long, and was really a settling-in period. The common expression was 'getting your pit eyes'. Within a week or two at the most you were soon elevated to the status of either a pony driver or haulage hand. If the former, it was an opportunity to make a new friend, the pit pony, and real pals, as we used to call them, they were.

Ponies could find their way in the dark, and on many occasions I recall they would sense the danger of a falling roof; although you would urge them on they would not budge, and suddenly you would hear the roof falling. There was a mutual respect, even affection, that developed between boy and pony, and an effort was made to keep the same pony to the one boy. When confidence and understanding had been established you became really attached to each other. A bit of green grass which we often took from the surface to them was a luxury the ponies relished and enjoyed. I suppose it reminded them of their natural habitat. I often wondered what their feelings were and what they would have said, had they been articulate, about the darkness and dangers, and the unnatural life they had to endure.

I thought the transfer from the surface to underground wonderful for it meant an increase from one and threepence

15

per day to two shillings, and to take home a golden coin of half a sovereign and a one shilling piece, providing of course you had worked six days, was thought marvellous. This was before 1914. At the outbreak of war, gold coins were withdrawn from circulation, and after almost sixty years have not reappeared. Every quarter the wage rate was increased by two pence per day, one shilling per week; by the time you were seventeen you would be receiving four shillings a day—twenty-four shillings for a six-day week. There were many times, owing to lack of orders, that the pit, particularly during the summer months, would work only three or four days a week, and, of course, 'no work, no pay'—there was no guaranteed week at that time. You could, and did, go to the pit every day, but at the end of the week, might have worked only three days. The pit knocked off at quarter time or half-way through the shift many days during the week, owing to lack of orders or a breakdown of machinery. There was also a custom in the case of a fatality—and this unfortunately often happened—that the pit ceased to work for the remainder of the shift. To have continued working after a fatality would have been sacrilege; stopping was a token of respect and sympathy for a comrade whose life had been prematurely ended, casting a shadow over the whole of the pit.

The first Friday (pay day) after the day of the tragedy there would always be a collection in the pit-yard for the dependants. Compensation was meagre: in the case of a man who left no dependents, only funeral expenses up to a maximum of fifteen pounds; for a widow not more than two hundred pounds; for a widow with dependant children not more than seven hundred pounds. The amounts were paid into Court, and the judge of the County Court decided how much should be paid to the widow every month until the sum was exhausted. It was often remarked that the price of the life of a man who had no dependants was not even the cost of purchasing one of the ponies for work in the pit.

At seventeen, three years after starting work underground, the moment arrived for me to begin working at the coal-face, an arduous and dangerous job.

Fifty years ago, there were no machines in the pit, and

every ounce of coal was obtained by a hand tool called a pick, and loaded by hand with a screen or fork into tubs. By this process the small coal of less than two inches had to be thrown into the goaf or gob. Over the years, millions of tons of this small coal were lost for ever. The reason given was that there was no market for it. For each ton produced and sent to the surface the price paid by the owners was two shillings and sixpence; in the contract agreed between the owners and the Union, the price included building stone, roof supports, setting wooden roof supports, and doing a certain amount of ripping and making the gateways higher. Thus there was a lot of work in addition to the actual coal getting and loading the tubs—all of which was included in the two shillings and sixpence per ton. Mental alertness and physical strength and endurance were needed at the coal-face; it was a job which involved wrestling with nature, and often I thought how reluctant nature was to give up her treasure, and in the process she exacted a heavy toll in the form of accidents, explosions, and disease of the lungs by the inhalation of dust. The price of coal in terms of life and limb down the years has been a heavy one.

From 1914 to 1926 I was a coal-face worker, working in five foot and two foot seams. I consider myself very fortunate to have escaped serious injury. Many old pals were less fortunate, some of whom received fatal injuries. Miners are a courageous, hard-working body of men, with a real sense of humour. Let me give you an example: John Nolan was being questioned as to why he had been absent the previous day. 'Ah,' said John, 'walking along the pit lane, the wind blowing in my face like hell, although struggling, I was unable to light my pipe, the last before reaching the pit. You see, boys, I turned round, kept walking and was home before I found out I was travelling in the wrong direction.' Sharing their trials and disappointments (and there were many) but also their triumphs, and not least their company and fellowship has been a privilege and honour for me.

I had been at the pit for four years and was seventeen when I experienced the first national strike—the forerunner of many to follow. It was 1912 and the whole of the British coal-field came to a stop. The miners were on strike to establish a minimum daily wage for the piece-rate workers, the men who actually produced the coal. If the coal was hard and geological conditions bad, miners on piecework would, after a week's hard work, have a wage packet of a few shillings only to take home. The wage was determined by the amount of coal produced and sent to the surface. The owners of the pits were under no other obligation except to pay on the tonnage sent out of the pit. The strike lasted six weeks and the outcome was that Mr Asquith's Liberal Government passed a Bill through Parliament giving legal effect to a miners' minimum wage for piece-rate workers. It was a triumph as well as a necessity.

Nine years afterwards, in 1921, there was another national strike by the miners and it lasted thirteen weeks. In this stoppage, as in 1912, I took no official part but I attended the meetings and was one of many thousands who responded to the call of the Miners' Federation and had confidence in the officials who conducted the negotiations.

It was a lovely summer, ideal weather for cricket and outdoor games. I remember it was the year of the first post-war cricket Tests, and the Australians were here. What a team they brought under the captaincy of Warwick Armstrong! I saw the first Test at Trent Bridge, Nottingham, but the outstanding memory I have was of seeing Charles McCartney score 346 runs against Nottinghamshire. What an innings it was, in one day!

One week before the stoppage began, I married; it was Easter Saturday, 26 March. The pit had the usual Easter holiday, from the Good Friday to the following Tuesday, without pay. The pit started work on the Wednesday, worked three days, and then there was a three months' strike. That was the beginning of my married life!

There was little strike pay, just a few shillings a week. My wife continued working, at this time as a shop assistant. She had left the mill where, from leaving school, she had worked as a ring-frame spinner. It was fortunate for us, compared with others, and we were able to avoid accumulating debts. The strike ended and we went back to work in the darkness and dangers of the pit, after three months of glorious sunshine. Now everybody, both industry and domestic consumers, was crying out for coal. Stocks, which had been considerable at the beginning of the stoppage, were depleted and the immediate prospect of full-time working for a time, at any rate, was rosy.

The prosperity was transient. Only five years went by before 1926 and the miners were locked out. The pits were only to be opened on new terms of contract, longer hours and a reduction of wages. This was strongly resisted by the miners, and on 1 May 1926 there began the longest and most formidable national stoppage in the history of coal-mining in Britain.

I shall return in another chapter to the struggle of 1926 and its aftermath, both because of the personal implications, and what it meant for the Miners' Union, particularly in the Nottinghamshire coal-field. One thing can clearly be seen, sticking out like a sore thumb : the mining industry from 1912 and earlier, up to the outbreak of the Second World War in 1939, was the cock-pit of economic struggle.

CHAPTER IV

Sunday School and Chapel

Attendance at a Sunday School, certainly up to the end of the First World War, was common practice in our close compact communities. A large number of mining villages were remote and somewhat isolated. Mansfield Woodhouse was adjacent to the town of Mansfield and was not so remote as some of the areas in Nottinghamshire where new pits had been sunk. But further east of Mansfield, where mining operations started from 1912 on an extensive scale, the new communities were more remote and isolated. Small rural villages like Edwinstowe, Welbeck, Ollerton and Bilsthorpe grew like mushrooms. Remoteness and isolation, in some degree, was the lot of all, for communications and transport were neither speedy nor frequent. Because of these circumstances, Sunday School and Chapel were the centre of the mining communities who by upbringing had been for generations radical nonconformists.

The number of Trade Union Leaders and Parliamentarians who had their training in the Methodist Sunday Schools and Chapels is legion!

Although attendance at Sunday School was voluntary, there were only a few children who did not attend either one of the Methodist or Church of England Sunday Schools in Mansfield Woodhouse. The ethical tuition and the standard of conduct set by the Superintendents and teachers, the majority of whom were miners and their wives, were very high. There was one great day every year: the Sunday School Anniversary. Everybody hoped for, and some even offered a prayer for, a fine day. It was a great occasion for the children, who sat on a platform reaching from floor to ceiling, in their new clothes:

their annual new outfit, only worn on Sundays until the following Anniversary day, when it became second best. The children sang and gave their recitations. It was indeed their day, and with people coming from neighbouring villages, some on bicycles, many on foot—Aunties and Uncles and Grandparents—it was a meeting place. Maybe they would not meet again for months. There was a preacher, of course, to conduct the Anniversary Service, but he was in the background. Nobody must overshadow the children; it was their day and mighty proud they were to be on the platform! All the parents made a special effort to be there, even those who attended chapel very infrequently. Many of them had sat on the same platform as their children. It was indeed a day of nostalgic memories.

The chatter outside after the service was confined to two topics: how well the children had done and how nice they were to the eye, and the amount of the collection. No concert at the Albert or Royal Festival Halls could give greater joy than the children gave in the Village Chapel on Anniversary day. For a few years up to 1914 there was also the Annual Sunday School Demonstration on Whitsuntide Monday. The scholars of the Methodist and Church of England Sunday Schools would parade through the streets; there were banners, tableaux and bands, and the whole population was on the streets.

One memory I retain which is not a pleasant one. I have thought a lot about the incident since the deliberation on the question of unity between the Anglicans and the Methodists. At the inception of the Demonstration at Mansfield Woodhouse the question of precedence was agreed. For the first one, the Anglican Sunday School was to head the procession, and in the following years all were to move up by an agreed rota. This meant that at the second Demonstration the Anglican Sunday School would be last in the procession. It is sad to relate that the Anglican School walked in the Demonstration only once—when it was first in the procession! It was, as I see it, an unfortunate episode, and did not help the relationships between the Anglicans and the nonconformists. Happily the passage of time has been a great healer.

In retrospect I must admit Sunday School did not mean a

lot to me until I was twelve years old. For this I am sure I am myself to blame. I feel I was bored, and reluctant to cooperate; possibly restless, and wanting something the Sunday School did not seem to offer. The responsibility for this is mine alone, for the teachers were all kind and helpful.

When I was twelve or thirteen years old, the Superintendent of the Sunday School, Mr Albert Fells, took on the responsibility of taking under his guidance this particular age group. Reflecting upon this, I am now certain and have been for many years, that there was a transformation in my attitude from that time. My interest was awakened and I became more receptive to what he had to say. Whether it was a silent conversion, an awakening, or the setting of a new course, I do not know, but there was a disposition to listen to this good, gentle, patient man. He was deeply religious and his life and the way he lived attracted me. What he was was more than what he said. He was a good radical and deeply interested in social and political questions, of which I knew so little. He talked to us lads much more about social matters and peace than theology. He knew the Bible quite well, but was more interested in the social implications of the Christian religion than theology.

During the South African war he must have been pro-Boer like Lloyd George, of whom he was a great admirer. I remember as if it was only yesterday his describing a visit of the Reverend Samuel Chadwick to the mother chapel of the Mansfield Wesleyan circuit. 'My lads,' he said during his sermon, 'if six men had been shot there would not have been a Boer War!' At the time, I was mystified and somewhat horrified, but later I came to agree with what he said. But it was many years before Samuel Chadwick was invited again to the mother chapel.

On another occasion he was talking to us on the oft quoted words of Jesus: 'Lay not up for yourselves treasures upon earth.' He went on to describe the qualities of a follower of the carpenter of Nazareth as character and integrity which he said were more important than anything else in the world, and he ended his talk by saying, 'My lads, remember they don't put pockets in shrouds!' The life of this good man, a hard-working miner with very little of this world's possessions, had a profound influence upon me. I am sure, on reflection, that this man was the person responsible for the turning-point at this early period of my life. I have, from my early teens, been grateful for his influence and I revere his memory. With deep and abiding gratitude I pay this tribute to him with humility and sincerity.

During the early part of the present century there was little choice in finding an avenue for youthful propensities. The area was restricted; communications were limited; the greater part of life was spent at the pit. I have no regrets that at that time I chose the chapel where I could be useful and improve my approach to life.

I was a member of the Band of Hope. This national organization was ancillary to the Sunday School where temperance in one sphere, the taking of alcohol, was encouraged. We referred to membership of the Band of Hope as having 'signed th pledge'—to refrain from taking alcohol—and the label of teetotallers was applied to the members of the Band of Hope. With rare gusto we used to sing at every meeting, 'My drink is water bright, from the crystal spring.' The addresses at every meeting were about the evil of 'strong drink'. Every time we gathered together we sang : 'Wine is a mocker, strong drink is raging.' The Band of Hope organization inside the Methodist Chapels was the bastion of teetotalism and it was regarded as a sin to indulge in strong drink in the time of my youth.

The Alliance of Honour and the Wesley Guild were two branches of the chapel catering for young people, and very useful they were. They too were organized nationally. The former was geared to the propagation of bodily health and cleanliness, and instruction on matters of sex education. Membership was open to both sexes. The literature published was instructive. Two of the books I still recall, by Dr Sylvanus Stall, were *What a Young Man Ought to Know* and *What a Young Woman Ought to Know*. I still have them on my bookshelves.

Sex education was approached with trepidation. There was hesitation and embarrassment, and great reluctance on the

part of the Sunday School and Chapel to enlighten young
people on matters of sex; emotions without knowledge were
common among young people. The Alliance of Honour did
a good job at that time. The media through which its work
was done was the Sunday School and Chapel, and many
young people were grateful for the information, both oral and
that published by the organization.

The Wesley Guild was an innovation; in the Primitive
Methodist Chapel there was an equivalent organization, the
Christian Endeavour, catering mainly for young people in the
Primitive Methodists. This, of course, was before Methodist
Unity. Both organizations in their respective denominations
did good work among young people. They were branches of
the Chapel interested not only in devotional matters, but in
literary and cultural subjects. An opportunity was provided
for young people to meet, make friends and establish contacts—some of which have remained constant. Although some
have gone their different ways and engaged in different pur-
suits, valuable friendships and contacts began in these organizations in the Chapels.

The organizations and the activities of the Chapel became
part of my life and meant much to me. I was restless and
unable to stand still. I was in a hurry, and was convinced the
Chapel was the instrument through which my dreams could
become realities. I was preoccupied with a longing and desire
to acquire knowledge in the sphere of Christian ethics and
standards. The field was limited and the opportunities few for
so much time was spent at the pit, but in what time there was
I began to read books of a devotional character.

I had now reached the age of fourteen; the little leisure
time available I spent in the activities of the Chapel, also taking part in the weekly class and prayer meetings. The Methodists were aware how important the weekly gathering of the
Chapel members were and the class meeting was an integral
part of Methodist activities. It was where the weekly dues
were paid, and, every quarter, each member was given a
ticket of membership signed by the Minister. There was no
Methodist Chapel without its class meeting and leader. It was
a useful institution, providing a collective opportunity for all

to relate their experiences and join in communal fellowship. Attendance at and being a member of the class meeting was the symbol of membership and the means of measuring the numerical membership of the Wesleyan Methodists throughout the nation. Up to 1914 Methodism was a force to be reckoned with. In fact, all the nonconformist chapels were very influential; and they had great preachers and lecturers who would draw great crowds to the services.

The local lay preachers were in great demand. In my youth they were all men. Without them it would have been impossible to have carried on with the weekly Sunday services. At the age of fifteen I was asked to give my first address to the Wesley Guild. On reflection, I can only assume that someone thought there was some potential in me for public speaking; it was not myself—I recoiled from the idea. I was, however, persuaded to undertake what for me was a big task. Everyone begins somewhere at some time it is said. I can only think by way of encouragement that big rivers, before entering the sea, have a beginning; at their source, they are only a trickle. 'Have a try!' the members said. 'Failure at the first shot is no disgrace. We shall be there to encourage.'

I approached this new venture with hesitation and trepidation. I recall the text upon which I based my remarks: 'Ye must be born again'. Apart from relating the story, and the circumstances under which they were spoken, I had little more to offer, and I felt it was not a good effort, but I received not only advice but encouragement from the members and was urged to go on. Had it not been for this, it might have been not only my first but also my last effort. The members were, or appeared to be, more pleased with the adventure than I was myself. So, undaunted, I continued, and it was the beginning, the first faltering step towards becoming a Methodist lay preacher. From this I had an intuition that this was my role in the Chapel, and becoming almost certain that this was the way for me, I took up the task with plenty of enthusiasm.

After a long and arduous day working underground, it was an effort to read and study the recommended books. Even now, after the passing of so many years, there are two I remember very well: Clapperton's book on theology and John Wesley's *Fifty-three Sermons*—pretty hard going, dealing as they did with imponderables; certainly not entertaining reading, but necessary in order to pass the examination to quality as a lay preacher.

I do recall taking my first service alone. This was an ordeal. It was at the village Wesleyan Chapel at Kneesall, near Newark in Nottinghamshire. My mother's sister with her husband and family lived there. They were devoted Methodists. My uncle Tom Padley was a lay preacher, and it was they who invited and prevailed upon me to take the plunge and take the service alone. It is now only a vague memory. What the text was and what I said about it I do not remember. I occasionally pass through the village, see the chapel and say to myself that in that building was the beginning of my efforts in the art of public speaking.

In 1911, now sixteen years old, I succeeded in the examination, having preached, to use Methodist terminology, my trial sermon. It was before at least one of the Ministers and two lay preachers. This was an ordeal. The comforting thought was that the examiners had passed through the same experience and although critical they were magnanimous. As well as the examiners there was the congregation, all of whom were sympathetic and helpful. They were also very appreciative that there was one more person coming forward to carry on this tradition of lay preachers. I passed the test and was accepted on the plan of the circuit as a fully accredited 'local preacher'.

I was given five to six appointments every quarter. This meant being away each alternate Sunday. The circuit was a big one in area and had a number of chapels, at least one in each town and village within the area of the circuit. There was no public transport to most of the places, and I had to walk to take an appointment or be taken by horse-drawn cab. To meet the cost of transport there was a circuit fund known as the 'local preacher's horse hire fund'. This was contributed to by occasional collections at all the chapels within the circuit.

There were few opportunities for recreation. I found much time was needed for preparing the addresses during the week, and the whole of the Sunday was taken up by travelling and taking the services. It was a busy life, and full of interest. I found it enjoyable and satisfying and was spurred on with the thought that I was making a contribution towards making the world a better place. I met many people and made many new friends; my small personal world was expanding and new horizons were coming into view. I was privileged to preach in every chapel in the circuit except the one which was regarded as the head, or the mother chapel. At that time, this chapel was almost the exclusive preserve of the ordained ministers; it was only very occasionally that one of the local preachers was appointed to take the service there. There was a fine body of locals on the plan : miners, agricultural and factory workers, school-teachers and business men, many of whom had a natural flair for oratory, but only a few of them graced the pulpit of the head chapel. This was an unjustified snobbery and was resented by the local preachers.

The year 1914 was a sad year : it heralded the outbreak of war. Under these new circumstances I began to widen the scope of my reading. During the next two or three years I became not only interested in but also absorbed by the writings of George Lansbury, the Reverand W. E. Orchard, E. D. Morel and many others, all of whom were in opposition to the war, either on Christian, pacifist, or political grounds. Of the latter I knew little. One of the books which I read in 1916 made a great impression on me—it was E. D. Morel's *Ten Years of Secret Diplomacy*. There was also the literature of the Fellowship of Reconciliation. All this I felt was nearer to Christian ethics than the general attitude of the Church. At that time war and even the thought of it was abhorrent, not only to myself as a practising Christian, but to almost everybody. I finally decided to be an objector as a Christian.

The mining industry was a reserved occupation. In 1918 there was a 'comb-out'. I was included. I was sent 'calling-up' papers to which I did not respond. Consequently I was arrested and court-martialled and sent to Wormwood Scrubs prison. This was a strange experience. The confinement and the absence of social and personal contact were depressing and disturbing. There were hundreds of men there, but no one you were allowed to speak to. There were a few pals there who had taken a similar stand but contact was impossible. It was work in the laundry and confinement in a single prison cell. The rule of no personal contact and no conversation was rigorously carried out. To me it was mental, not physical, punishment, and had it not been for a faith that kept the spirit buoyant, those few months would have been a hell.

The only contact with people was through books, which were not too liberally supplied. But the Bible was always there, and this I read assiduously, particularly the story of Joseph in prison, and of Nehemiah for whom the gallows had been prepared. Two other books I remember well, *God and My Neighbour* by Robert Blatchford and Darwin's *The Origin of Species*. These made me think, for they were a challenge to many of my orthodox beliefs and opinions, and to the fundamentalist position from a religious standpoint. Mentally I was going through a Gethsemane, revising my ideas about the orthodox pattern of religious teaching and belief. I was also experiencing a political awakening, and the need to apply Christian ethics and standards to our social and economic life.

The Independent Labour Party appealed to me in its work and propaganda and, in 1919, upon returning home, I joined this organization and became a declared socialist. I maintained my membership with the Chapel and continued on the plan as a lay preacher, but life was not easy. I felt resentment for among many of the members socialism was unacceptable. Also I had abandoned many of my beliefs in some of the traditional doctrines of the Chapel. In this process of mental change from the orthodoxy and fundamentalism in which I had been brought up and had a profound belief, the ground was shifting, and the social implications of Christianity were becoming more and more important.

In 1921 I resigned from the plan as a local preacher and soon afterwards my membership of the Chapel came to an end; and for the past fifty years I have not been actively identified with the chapel where my early life had been spent and where my early training began. Some of the chapel people were of the opinion that my leaving was a mistake. I recall some of my closest friends saying how sorry they were at my decision. My immediate predecessor in the House of Commons was Charles Brown, a lay preacher and an objector who was also imprisoned. I know many others who had an identical experience: links with the Chapel were broken, and their time and abilities were given to the socialist movement.

The old chapel in Mansfield Woodhouse is now closed. Its numbers declined and it was impossible to continue. The building has been sold and is now used as a hosiery factory. When passing it, as I do frequently, memories are still there, memories of individuals and of happy times as a scholar, a teacher in the Sunday School, and a preacher from the pulpit. In 1916 the Superintendent Minister of the circuit, the Reverend J. L. Webber (who I learned from a radio broadcast two years ago had reached the age of one hundred) asked me with the utmost persuasion to offer myself as a candidate for the Wesleyan Ministry. My thinking was beginning a process of change, and I was not attracted by the proposition and so declined the offer. My life would have been different—certainly it would have been more proscribed—whether more useful, who knows. On reflection, I do not think so, and consequently I have no regrets for the wider experiences including plenty of rough and tumble which have been my life. But I am not unmindful of the influence of Methodism in my early life, and the help of so many fine and noble people who were at the time its pillars. To this day I have memories of the chapel and its people; I still recognize my indebtedness to its influence and the opportunities for service it provided and I still enjoy listening to and joining in the singing of the hymns.

CHAPTER V

Trade Union Activity

After the mining stoppage of 1921 my interest in the Trade
Union movement grew, and my activities increased. I began
to attend the Branch or Lodge meetings, taking part in the
discussions. The President of the Branch and the Delegate to
the county headquarters were two fine men who were always
helpful; they were not mean in their words of encouragement
to those who were younger. The progress of the Union, called
the Nottinghamshire Miners' Association, a part of the Miners'
Federation of Great Britain, was of great concern to them.
Both the President and Delegate were old enough to have
taken part in the early struggles of the Union for recognition.
These two men, Tom Knapton and Jesse Farmilo, to whom I
shall refer later, played a major part in the activities of the
Branch. There were others, the Secretary and the committee
men, whose collective effort was responsible for the activities of
the Branch according to the rules of the County Association.
The Miners' Union has always been a democratic organization, and every member was entitled to participate in its
business, to express his point of view and to decide by vote
whom the officials should be, not only at the individual pits
but all along the line, including the national officials. At the
time to which I am referring the late Robert Smillie and the
late Frank Hodges were President and Secretary respectively
of the Miners' Federation and had been elected by the votes
of the miners throughout the British coal-field.

In 1923 I was elected to the Branch Committee and in
1924 or 1925, having served a brief apprenticeship in this
capacity, I was elected the Secretary of the Branch. These
elections were by individual ballot at the pit-head. At this

time the Union was not prosperous financially. Recovery from the 1921 stoppage was only just beginning. Debts had been incurred and loans had been raised; the local Co-operative Society had been good to the Union and to the miners in this respect. To liquidate the debts, levies additional to the usual weekly contributions were imposed on individual members, in spite of their low wages, in order to make the Union solvent, and to begin to build up its funds for any emergency that might arise.

It was anybody's guess when the next crisis might occur. Experience had bitten deeply. The short prosperity after the 1921 stoppage had evaporated : the owners of the pits were insisting that the industry was in a bad way and that costs of production, by which they meant wages, would have to be reduced.

In 1925, clouds of uncertainty were gathering, and all attempts to negotiate a settlement between the coal owners and the Miners' Federation failed. The Government came forward with a subsidy of £25 million, and, as a result, but for the moment only, a stoppage was averted. This armistice, for that is what in reality it was, turned out to be short-lived. However, negotiations continued. It was only a breathing space for the Government, the miners, and the owners. In a few short months there was stalemate. The stoppage could have happened in 1925; it had only been postponed a few months. The owners were prepared only to keep open the pits on new terms of longer hours and reduced wages. The miners were not prepared to accept reduced wages, and certainly not a lengthening of the working day. On the first day of May 1926, the storm broke and a long, bitter struggle began. This was my first experience of a national stoppage as a local Branch official.

There was elation that the wider Trade Union movement, the T.U.C., was with the miners, and it called a General Strike in support. This collapsed after nine days, and the miners struggled on alone, determined to resist the lengthening of the working day, and a reduction in wage rates. 'Not a minute on the day, nor a penny off the pay' was a slogan epitomizing the miners' case. It was a phrase coined by the late A. J. Cook

31

who was the Secretary of the Miners' Federation, having succeeded the late Frank Hodges. The slogan caught on: it was easy to remember and became most popular among the miners. Whatever was said from the public platform at the many meetings, it was all based on the slogan. When miners were asked why they were locked out, it was so easy to answer, the slogan was there: 'Not a minute on, not a penny off.'

The miners' stoppage in 1926 was not a strike by the miners—they were locked out by the owners. The pits, after 30 April 1926, were open for work only on the terms offered. It was a formidable struggle: inflexibility on the part of the coal owners, determination by the miners to resist the newly-offered conditions. I naturally saw the national struggle intimately from the point of view of the Nottinghamshire pits. The coffers of the Nottinghamshire miners were low and there was little pay from Union funds. Financially the prospect was bleak but this did not deter the miners in their resistance to a lowering of their standards. There was a one hundred per cent response not only in Nottinghamshire, but throughout the British coal-field.

The beginning of the stoppage coincided with the May Day demonstration and meeting in Mansfield. What a demonstration! My memory of it is still fresh. It was a blazing hot day, and it appeared that the major part of the population of the town and the surrounding mining communities was either on the streets or in the parade itself. I can recall no other time when the streets of Mansfield were so filled with people. In the parade every Trade Union was there, and the turn-out of individual members walking behind their banners was a magnificent sight. At this stage the General Strike was only one day old, but not only the miners, but also every worker was involved. The local strike committee had been formed of people connected with all the Trade Unions in the town. Great credit is due to German Abbott who did an excellent job, organizing and co-ordinating the various activities. It was a new experience for everybody; nothing like this had happened before. There were no trains and little road transport. What there was was confined to those issued with permits. There were no newspapers and no communications of any kind except by couriers, who went from place to place delivering messages, some on foot, some on bicycles. Pits, factories, transport, all communications media stopped; on the other hand, the strike committee was working round the clock, and this unprecedented situation lasted for nine days, at the end of which the miners were on their own for the General Strike had been called off.

There were disappointment and recriminations but these were matched with determination among the miners to go on, and so they did. The finances of the Notts Miners' Association were low and there was no prospect of any financial benefit from the Union funds. Assistance came from various sources including the Trade Union movement of the Soviet Union of Russia. The gesture was appreciated, but among so many in the British coal-field, the number at the time being in the region of one million, it meant very little to the individual. Nevertheless in total it was a handsome, generous contribution. The main source of income was from the Boards of Guardians in the form of relief on loan. Thousands of pounds of debt were incurred by the miners in the Mansfield area to the Mansfield Board of Guardians. People do not realize today that at the end of the stoppage on the return to work, deductions from the wage packets were made to repay the money.

From the beginning of the stoppage, it was realized something would have to be done for the children, and soup kitchens were set up. Funds were limited, and appeals to local traders were made. Also many of the miners who were keen gardeners and had allotments helped considerably. Each community made itself responsible for organizing the kitchens and providing at least one meal a day for the children. The Trade Union branch had no premises at which the meals to the children could be served, but the churches were very co-operative, and allowed their Sunday Schools to be used for this purpose.

In Mansfield Woodhouse the local Labour Party (the majority of whose members were miners and their wives) was the instrument for most of the activities. There was a wonderful spirit among them: they prepared, cooked, and served the meals to the children. It was to them a labour of love and they felt it was their part in the struggle of their husbands. Really, it had to be seen to be believed. Fortunately, the weather was wonderful and at its majestic best. The miners used to say with the dawn of another day, that the Lord was on their side. The majority of us knew little about cyclones, anti-cyclones and depressions and there was no regular weather forecast. A warm spell just came, and how delighted we were to have the hot, sunny days for so long! The summer of 1926, I think, was the best I have experienced: long sunny days for many weeks. We were poor financially but the kind of weather we had was some compensation — indeed a blessing, and it helped us in our determination.

I have one particular memory that is still fresh: the bringing of the pit ponies to the surface. At Sherwood pit, 250 were brought up. This was a big undertaking as there could be only one pony on each deck of the two-decked cage. Getting them on at the pit bottom and off at the surface was quite a problem. When they arrived at the surface they were led to an enclosed field adjacent to the pit and when they were released, they ran and gambolled like new-born lambs. The light and the sun and the green of the field were things they had forgotten for many of them had not experienced them since 1921. There were ten pits within a radius of five miles of Mansfield. The number of the ponies brought from underground in this small area would be, at a minimum, 2,000. Many of the pony drivers watched the proceedings, and paid daily visits to the fields to see and have a word with the ponies they were responsible for when at work, and the ponies knew the link of friendship was still there.

This aspect of the stoppage was pleasurable to everybody, but there was a lot of work to be done, and this fell to the branch officials who organized meetings. Getting the men together was very important. At the initial stage it was necessary to have a register of all the men, to ascertain whether they were married and, if so, the number of their dependant children. This was important for the organization of the paying out of any money that came from the headquarters of the Union. This task was the responsibility of the Secretary and

Treasurer of each branch. Even this was not without its funny side. I said to one of our members, a man I knew well, when he arrived at the table, 'Now, Sam, how many children?' He replied, 'Three in England and there may be some in India.' He had been in His Majesty's Army, and as a soldier had spent a number of years in India!

Advertising the meetings was easily done for one of the members, golden-voiced Charlie Cross, took on the job of going round with a bell as the printing of leaflets was too expensive. Charlie became the equivalent of the Town Crier. After he had been round with the bell, there was no doubt that the meeting would be a numerical success. In the early 1930's Charlie Cross was killed in the pit by a fall of roof, one of many victims over the years. How can the price of coal be measured?

Most of the meetings were in the open, in the market-square or one of the local Local Authority's recreation grounds, willingly and generously lent. There were many local speakers, men who could take the platform at a moment's notice, and who were able and competent to argue the miners' case and to keep alive the spirit of determination. Owen Ford, a stalwart expert in the art of expression, succeeded on many occasions in retaining the interest of the miners. He was a wonderful orator, and was the platform idol of the miners. At the time of writing he is alive, almost ninety years old and enjoying a well-earned retirement.

Other local speakers gracing the platform were William Bayliss, Val. Coleman, Frank Varley, M.P., and George Spencer, M.P. of the Nottinghamshire Miners, all of whom were county officials. To many of the meetings came Harry Hicken, John Spencer, and Oliver Wright from the adjoining coal-field of Derbyshire. Meetings were so numerous that every day there were often more than one and the task of providing speakers was not easy, but the local orators were always at the ready. Men such as Tom Pembleton, Harry Alcock, German Abbott (all three check-weighmen at Rufford), William Smith, Alec. Norris, James Cantrill, Jesse Farmilo, Tom Knapton, all did a magnificent job on the platform in keeping the men in good heart. Many others undertook less spectacular jobs, ad-

mitting with modesty that they had no pretensions to public
speaking but acting as chairmen instead. Their presence on
the platforms was of great value. Almost fifty years have
passed, and most of those whose names I have mentioned, and
many others, have passed on, but I still cherish their comrade-
ship and fellowship. They were the salt of the earth, dedicated
to the cause of maintaining the miners' standards.

Speakers from other mining areas graced the local platforms.
I recall two meetings in particular. One was in the Y.M.C.A.
Hall in Mansfield, the other in the open air in Bulwell Forest
in the city of Nottingham. This latter meeting was both for
the county of Nottinghamshire and for Derbyshire as well. It
was convenient for both coal-fields; some parts of Derbyshire
were nearer to the Forest than some parts of Nottinghamshire.
It was fourteen miles from Mansfield. Hundreds of men and
women from the Mansfield area made the journey to Bulwell.
How they got there was their own affair, for motor cars
amongst miners were undreamed-of luxuries in 1926. There
was very little road transport. Neither before nor since have
I witnessed such a crowd, not even at a football match. It is
impossible to state the number accurately. The generally
agreed estimate was 80,000 to 100,000. From all parts of the
Nottinghamshire and Derbyshire coal-fields they came. The
speaker was A. J. Cook, the Miners' National Secretary. Off
came his coat and, with a voice affected by addressing so many
meetings, he began, like the crusader he was. What a sight it
was, and what an experience! Thousands did not hear a word,
for there were no loudspeakers and amplifiers at that time.
Despite this, everybody agreed it was worth the journey. There
was no work the following day, no need to rise at 4 a.m. or
5 a.m. and what did the long haul home matter, even if it
took all night! A meeting to be addressed by A. J. Cook was
a magnet to the miners and their wives, for he had become
their idol.

The meeting in Mansfield was to be addressed by two men
from the South Wales coal-field, Tom Richards and Aneurin
Bevan. The former had served the miners in Wales and
throughout the British coal-field for many years. He was well
known by name, and highly respected. Aneurin Bevan was of

the younger generation, at this time in his middle twenties and unknown outside Wales. At the end of the meeting, I recall an old friend saying to me, 'What a speaker! At no time have I had such pleasure in listening. There is a future Prime Minister if ever there was one in the making!' And how nearly right he was! At that time it was the last of my thoughts that I should get to know Aneurin so well, and be with him in the House of Commons.

It was my privilege to speak at many meetings in the coal-fields of Nottinghamshire and Derbyshire. There was a clamour for meetings, which provided the opportunities to meet collectively and to be informed of the latest position. If there had not been a meeting for two or three days one was inundated with questions like, 'When are we having a meeting?' or 'When and where is the next?' There was an insatiable appetite to hear the spoken word.

At one of the meetings in the Y.M.C.A. Hall in Mansfield I was one of the speakers. The attraction, A. J. Cook, was to speak also, and the hall was packed to more than capacity. A. J. Cook was never punctual if he had a previous engagement and had had difficulty in getting away. I have known him to be still at the previous meeting anything up to two hours after the next meeting has started.

At the meeting referred to, the Chairman whispered to me when I was speaking that I had to keep going until Mr Cook arrived. This I did but it seemed an eternity. He eventually arrived, however, much to my great relief, and no doubt to the relief of everyone in the Hall! My compensation was that the men and women were patient, tolerant and understanding. Their reward was that the man whom they had come to see and hear had arrived.

At the meetings, whether in a building or in the open, it was common practice for the police to be present and sometimes representatives of the colliery management. At a meeting in the Y.M.C.A. Hall the Chairman whispered to me while I was speaking and told me that the manager of one of the local pits was in the audience and taking notes. My immediate reaction was that he would use my words in evidence against me in the future. Another meeting I recall in this respect was held in the picture house at Mansfield Wood-house, not a palatial place. From the platform, it was like looking down a long, dark tunnel, and it was difficult to pick out who was among the audience. I was one of the speakers. The following day I was informed that the Superintendent of Police wanted to see me. I duly and promptly went to the police station, with more curiosity than apprehension, not knowing what the proposed interview was to be about. He asked if I had made certain statements the previous day that could be interpreted as a breach of the peace, and on which a charge could be made. This I denied and asked if he had in front of him a shorthand report. He admitted he had not. I knew then that no charge could be made, and in this I was right, for he said, 'That is all. Be a good lad, and be careful what you say or there may be consequences!'

The days grew into weeks, and the weeks into months. There was no visible sign how and when the stoppage would end. The miners were feeling that not only the coal owners but the Government and the establishment generally were against them, and there was justification for this. The miners' stoppage of 1926 will be remembered by my generation while memory lasts. The struggle itself, and all the circumstances, made a deep and abiding impression. Today when you meet people who actively participated in the struggle, they will reminisce and say, although it was a long time ago, 'I still remember'.

The circumstances of 1926 provided opportunities among the miners for platform, administrative and organizational ability, and great talent was revealed and made use of. In the years to follow I can think of many whose ability has been used in the Union and as representatives on Local Authorities. What they did in 1926 was the beginning of many useful years in public life.

For three or four months there was a hundred per cent solidarity and unity, and the fervour and enthusiasm over this long period remained firm, but there appeared a source of irritation. On the western side of Mansfield, in the Erewash valley, there was coal near the surface and, to use a local phrase, outcropping began; some of the miners began working there and this was regarded as a source of irritation and a breaking of the ranks. It led to clashes and ugly scenes. Those participating were looked upon as black-legs. The owners in Nottinghamshire were throwing open the pits on terms more favourable than those offered before the beginning of the stoppage. Here was a situation of a coal famine: stocks had gone and everybody, industry and domestic consumers, were in a bad way. The Mining Association of Great Britain would not negotiate on a national basis; it was left to the local county associations to negotiate with the county Miners' Unions.

By the end of August and the beginning of September, the drift back to work was spreading, not only locally but in the other coal-fields. This was disconcerting to all those who were determined to be loyal to the national organization, the Miners' Federation of Great Britain. This situation intensified the efforts both locally and nationally to persuade those who were drifting back to work to return to the ranks they had left. There was picketing and more meetings than at any time. Top ranking officials and speakers from all over the British coal-fields came to Nottinghamshire in the hope of stiffening resistance, and to demonstrate solidarity and unity with their comrades. The situation in Nottinghamshire brought great bitterness and disappointment not only to Branch officials but to many of the rank and file. To say it was an unpleasant situation is very temperate language. There were clashes between those who were still determined to resist and those who had drifted back to work, and the police had to take an active part. Lack of resources was affecting morale and determination, and, when the pits were thrown open, the relieving officers of the Boards of Guardians were not backward in telling all the recipients of relief that now there was work available they would be well advised to return to work. The management of the pits sent a notice to each individual employee that his job was available and if he wanted reinstatement in his pre-stoppage job and on the new terms of contract, he had better jump to it. They were told that if police protection was needed because of the pickets and fear of molestation, that also was available.

The moment had arrived when a determined effort was being made to sow the seeds of dissension in the ranks, and break the strike; and in Nottinghamshire it produced results. The circumstances of semi-starvation, the fear among the men that their jobs would be taken, and the prospect of victimization and unemployment were strings pulling at their hearts, and the position worsened daily. Nottinghamshire was regarded in other parts of the coal-field as a black spot and the weakest link in the chain of the Miners' Federation of Great Britain. It was all too obvious by October that the battle was lost so far as Nottinghamshire was concerned. But there were pockets of resistance in every part of the county composed of men who said they were not prepared to bow the knee to Baal and to forsake the Miners' Federation.

The struggle so far as the Federation was concerned continued until 19 November when the stoppage was called off nationally. The county districts of the Union were recommended to enter into negotiations with the coal owners locally. After seven months' struggle for a national settlement the dream was shattered. The owners and the Government had triumphed. The men were beaten but they were certainly not disgraced; they were beaten not through lack of courage and spirit, nor because their cause was not right and just, but because economic and political forces were too strong. The official ending of the 'Lock-Out' was not the end but the beginning of a long, hard journey for the Miners' Federation, characterized by victimization and unemployment for many individuals not only in Nottinghamshire, but throughout the British coal-field.

I vividly recall one experience, immediately the stoppage was officially called off, when I went with the President of the Branch, Tom Knapton, to see the under-manager for work. Tom was a fine character who had spent many years working underground. He was a good, experienced collier who could turn his hand to any job underground and a useful man to be employed in any colliery. He was one of the old school, steeped in Trade Unionism, outspoken and forthright, not only to the management but to the men as well. Both of us had worked at Sherwood for many years and together we went to see Mr Stirland, the under-manager, about starting work. We stood outside the office door. Before we entered, the General Manager of the company appeared. His manner and attitude were the negation of politeness. When he approached us, not only did he not speak, but he turned round, lifted his coat tails, and, to use the words of Jack London, he showed us that part of his anatomy constructed for the reception of kicks. With no feeling of shame, we were determined to see the under-manager about a job. We entered the office. The dialogue was brief and terse, and one could sense the atmosphere was not one of welcome. I am certain the under-manager would have preferred that we had stayed away. However, we asked about the chance of a start. The under-manager, who had known us for many years having had previous dealings with us about pit problems, was obviously embarrassed. There was no asking 'How are you?' or even a 'Good morning'. We could have been complete strangers. His eyes looking into a book, he said tersely 'Full up'. To every question put, we got the same answer: 'Full up'. He was not normally a man of few words. Of course we had had many arguments in past days when discussing pit problems, and he was then at no time lost for words, some of which were not to be found in a dictionary. On this occasion he had no disposition to argue. The sooner he saw the back of us the better he would be pleased. I remember saying to him, 'Suppose there comes a time when you are not "Full up", will there be any chance of a start?' I got the same reply: 'Full up.'

Beginning to feel exasperated at the brevity of his replies, I said: 'Well, Mr Stirland, it may not be easy to find a job, but you won't take our hands and tongues. We may find pastures new. Under the circumstances we know it will be difficult, but we shall have to hope and do the best we can.' At this stage he appeared to relent. The better side of his nature began to take control, and he began to thaw and became a little more articulate. 'Don't talk like that, Bernard! I have my job to do, and my instructions to carry out.' It was obvious that whatever his personal inclinations were, as under-manager, he was not free to employ anyone he wished. We left the office in no way surprised at the reception and the failure of our application for a job.

What did surprise us was that when we emerged from the

office to make our way home, we were met by two policemen who escorted us from the colliery premises on to the public highway, a distance of half a mile. This, I am sure, was at the request of the General Manager, who half an hour before had treated us so rudely, and by lifting his coat tails was in effect saying, 'talk to my bottom'. This final humiliation was beyond our comprehension. Although we had participated in the struggle and kept faith with the Miners' Federation, we knew we were beaten. The General Manager also knew this. This action was like rubbing our noses in the ground good and proper. Magnanimity in victory is a virtue, but this was sadly lacking. To be refused work was no surprise. The coal owners were expert at black-listing and needed no tuition in carrying it out, but to be treated in such a way was humiliating.

Tom Knapton, a great character, an ardent Primitive Methodist, a lay preacher, also a member of the Local Authority, held in high esteem by the general public, was humiliated beyond description. Although a strong man, he was overcome with indignant emotion. With a tremor in his voice, and tears in his eyes, he said, as we walked down the pit lane, the policemen by the side of us, 'What's tha' think of that, lad? The monkey!' At no time did I think the under-manager responsible for refusing us work. He had his orders from the top. They were the same throughout the British coal-field. At the end of this book I will relate an experience I had with the under-manager a few months before he died in 1942.

It was now within a few weeks of Christmas 1926. Re-sources were dwindling and prospects were bleak. Between 1921 and 1926, my wife and I had exercised care and we had saved as much as possible for two reasons: first to provide a home of our own (from the time of our marriage in 1921 we had shared a house with my parents); secondly we knew the economics of the coal industry were such that the flush of prosperity following the stoppage of 1921 would soon evaporate. When demand for coal diminished and stocks had been rebuilt, the short-lived prosperity of the industry would begin to degenerate. And so it was, in 1924, that there were signs of conflict again, and had it not been for a subsidy from the Government, the stoppage would have taken place in 1925; but this is another story, interesting and fascinating. The Baldwin Government saw the possibility of conflict, and the subsidy was the buying of time to prepare, should the worst happen.

During the succeeding nine months the Government took active steps by creating an organization called the O.M.S., the Organization for Maintenance of Supplies. All this preparation between the years 1924 to 1926 is now part of history and so much has been written about it that I do not propose to say more.

On reflection, I would not be guilty of an overstatement in saying that our total income for these months from the beginning of the stoppage in May to the official ending in November 1926 was not in excess of £10, possibly less. Pay from the Union was small, and I was unable to obtain relief from the Guardians because I was a member. I joined the queue with my comrades but I knew what the answer would be. As I arrived at the table at which the relieving officer sat, he said, 'Sorry, Mr Taylor, but as a member of the Board you are not eligible for relief.' This was no surprise. We made the most of the resources we had accumulated between 1921 and 1926 and a couple of endowment insurance policies had to be surrendered.

One incident I remember well on Christmas Eve 1926. Hearing a knock on the door, I opened it to find an unknown person with a box of chocolates for our son, now four years old. Handing it to me, he said, 'I am forbidden to say who the donor is. With his best wishes he has sent this as a gift.' To this day I have no idea who the donor of the chocolates was.

In 1925 I bought a plot of land with a view to building a house. I had plans prepared and arranged a mortgage with the local Co-operative Society. The builder took the first sod off the ground on the first day of the stoppage. What a coincidence! I had some apprehensions as to the wisdom of going on with the project but it was too late to draw back. Also there was the hope that the stoppage would soon be over. But it did not turn out like that. By another coincidence we took occupation of the house almost on the day of the official ending of the stoppage in November 1926. It was impossible to furnish the house as we would have liked. Finances were very limited so the place was sparsely furnished. But it was our first home, and we had been married five years!

Under the circumstances the new venture was not promising; our trials were just beginning and were to go on for a very long time. As the weeks and months went by, we were more hopeful than confident as to the future. Faced with a mortgage, and with monthly payments and rates, we decided to let part of the house to my wife's sister and her husband who had recently married. This arrangement eased the burden, and was indeed our salvation as it helped to meet our obligations financially.

In late December 1926, I decided to try for reinstatement at Sherwood pit again. I went to see the under-manager. The reception was no more cordial and the answer the same as the one a month earlier: 'Full up!' I was told I did not work there any more and it was obvious that reinstatement was out of the question. So far as I was concerned, the management could have inscribed on the office door, 'Ye who enter here abandon hope.' This applied throughout the Nottinghamshire and Derbyshire coal-fields not only to myself but to many other good comrades, especially to the lodge officials, who had taken an active part during the stoppage. The coal owners could have posted a notice at every one of their pits in respect of those whom they had decided not to re-employ: 'Vengeance is mine. I will repay.' This was a true reflection of their attitude and conduct towards some of the best and most talented men it has been my privilege to meet, good workmen and first-class experienced colliers. This calculated process of victimization denuded the industry of good men of character and integrity. Their only offence had been their loyalty to their Union and because of it they and their families paid a heavy price.

The beginning of my official capacity with the Union, the first rung of the ladder so to speak, was in December 1923 when I was nominated for a position on the Branch Committee. The decision was made by individual ballot of the

44

men. A few days afterwards it was Christmas Eve, the last working shift before the Christmas holidays of 1923.

It was always a welcome break; it is a long time to Christmas from the Bank Holiday break at the beginning of August. The hours of daylight in the last quarter of the calendar year become fewer, and the opportunity of seeing daylight is negligible at this time of the year. This year the part of the pit where I was working was two miles from the shaft bottom. From this part of the pit the men were always among the last to arrive at the pit bottom to be wound to the surface. On this day, 24 December, I and others stepped into the cage, singing, 'While Shepherds watched their flocks'—thankful we had thus far been spared to see the dawn of another Christmas. We arrived safely at the surface, trousers wet with sweat. We handed in our lamps at the lamp cabin and walked along the pit-yard, making for home. There were no pit-head baths at this time, and the washing and drying of trousers wet with sweat was done at home.

Coming in the opposite direction was the under-manager. I am sure he was relieved that all the men on the day shift had arrived safely at the surface. The under-manager asked me to go to his office for a chat. I was hungry, wet through with sweat, and tired. My first thoughts were, 'What now? What has gone wrong? Is this an inquest about something?' However, it turned out differently: no castigation, no inquest. I confess to a feeling of surprise and amazement as the dialogue continued.

'Well, Bernard, I have seen the result of the ballot and noticed you have been elected to the Lodge committee. Do you think you are taking the right course? I started in a similar way, but came to the conclusion I could be of a greater service this side of the table, so I obtained a deputy's certificate and became a deputy, continued my studies, obtained my second-class certificate and now I am under-manager.' I wondered where this was leading to and what it all meant. During the conversation, he made a reference to Ramsay MacDonald and the gift of a motor car from a biscuit firm. 'You know, they all have their price,' he said. At this I was nettled, and showed my annoyance, and wondered what he was getting at.

45

I am sure he had noticed my resentment for he said, 'I am sure your motives are good and commendable but think hard whether you are wise in the interest of your future.' He then said, 'You know Jack Ashmore?' 'Of course,' I said, 'you mean the Deputy.' 'Well, at the end of the month,' he said, 'he is retiring on a pension. I only wish you had your deputy's certificate, I would offer you his job.' At this point I could now see the real purpose of the interview. To his surprise I told him I had the certificate. Maybe I should have kept this from him, so that he would not have had to make the offer, and I would not have had to make the decision. I knew in my own mind at once that I would turn down the offer, but thought it wise to be diplomatic, so I said, 'In the event that I do not come to see you immediately after the Christmas holiday, you may take it that the answer is "no".' We parted that Christmas Eve good friends, wishing each other the season's compliments. I did not go to see him, and it was not my intention to accept the offer.

Three years were all too short as a local official, first as a member of the committee, and later as Secretary of the Lodge, before the stoppage of 1926. My work as Secretary was interesting and absorbing: keeping the contribution books and collecting the contributions at the Union office in the pit-yard, a facility provided by the management. All contributions were paid voluntarily at that time, not automatically deducted from wages as they are now and have been for the last twenty-five years. The major job was to get all the men into the Union. Many, after the stoppage of 1921, had fallen out of membership, and the task was not easy and by 1926 there was not one hundred per cent membership. There were the daily grievances and such problems as the price list difficulties of the piece-rate workers to be dealt with. These varied from district to district in the same pit, and were often the cause of dissatisfaction. Matters of compensation arising through accident and industrial disease, particularly nystagmus, seldom heard of today, also had to be dealt with. Fifty and more years ago, it was prevalent among miners: better illumination in the pits has removed this malady. It had unpleasant effects: oscillation of the eyeballs, and headaches. For some it ended employment underground and this raised questions of compensation. Dermatitis, an industrial disease, was a real bone of contention and dissatisfaction. There were many problems and the Trade Union played a big and important part in ironing out the difficulties. Many could be solved at pit level. Those that were insoluble locally were passed to the Area official. The Branch Secretary was an important part of the machinery.

It was an interesting job meeting people and discussing their problems and grievances with them. It was an experience to be valued. The book-keeping, correspondence, negotiating and dealing with men and women with problems have proved of inestimable worth over the years to me. I was full of enthusiasm and felt greatly privileged to have been elected as a Lodge Secretary, and endeavoured to serve my fellow men and comrades at the pit to the best of my ability. I had an inward satisfaction that I was making a contribution, however small, and in a limited capacity to Trade Unionism in which I had a profound belief. I inwardly felt it had a great part to play in national and international affairs, and there is now plenty of evidence to justify the belief I had fifty years ago, when I first became a Branch official of the Miners' Union at Sherwood pit.

CHAPTER VI

The Spencer Union

As a consequence of the drift back to work a new organization emerged in 1926, purporting to represent the men in the Nottinghamshire coal-field. This situation, welcomed and encouraged by the local coal owners, provided the opportunity for a few men who had been, and were, active in the Nottinghamshire Miners' Union to take advantage of seceding from the National Federation and forming this new Industrial Union. It was well known that they were not lacking in sympathy with non-political Trade Unionism, and had more enthusiasm for district than national agreements.

The man who became the spearhead and leader, Mr George Alfred Spencer, was one of the full-time officials of the Nottinghamshire Miners' Association, and had been for a number of years. He was also the Member of Parliament for the Broxtowe division of Nottinghamshire and had been from the first post-war election in 1918. He was a member of Parliament sponsored by the Miners' Federation. His action in forming this breakaway rival Union, meant that his long connection with the Miners' Federation was severed. He stayed in the House of Commons until the General Election of 1929 when he did not seek re-election. He was an able man; to deny this would be wrong. On the platform he was a good speaker, and very knowledgeable, particularly on Workmen's Compensation. I did not know him personally at the time of the breakaway. At this time, and before, his work and activities as an official of the Union were in the Erewash and the Leen Valleys of the county, and he was rarely in the Mansfield area. His action was bitterly resented among miners not only in the Nottinghamshire coal-field but throughout the country and the Trade Union movement generally.

The new Union, officially described as the Nottinghamshire and District Miners' Industrial Union was better known locally as the 'Spencer Union', and became widely known as such throughout the nation, particularly in Trade Union circles. It was known locally by other names, very uncomplimentary ones, the most common reference to it locally being 'The Gaffers' Union'. I do not propose to go into further detail of how and why it began, because books have already been written: Dr A. Griffin's *History of the Nottinghamshire Miners*, Dr Williams' *History of the Derbyshire Miners*, and R. Page Arnot's *History of the Miners' Federation*. All these works have something to say about the origin of the Spencer Union. My purpose in referring to it is to relate the effects and the conditions that prevailed for eleven years in the Nottinghamshire coal-field as an eye witness and a participant in the struggle.

With the official ending of the stoppage in 1926, the rise of the new rival Union, and the refusal of the Nottinghamshire coal owners to meet representatives of the Nottinghamshire Miners' Association, there was an unprecedented situation. A pledge had been given to the Spencer Union by the owners that it would be the only Union to be recognized as the negotiating body. Furthermore, the Nottinghamshire Miners' Association were not to be allowed on the colliery premises for any purpose, even for the collecting of the weekly contributions. This was a blow to the pride and prestige of the Nottinghamshire Miners' Association. The aim of the coal owners and the Spencer Union in this was to obliterate the Nottinghamshire Miners' Association and to destroy free Trade Unionism in the Nottinghamshire coal-field.

It proved to be a long drawn-out battle, for there were many miners not prepared to see the light of the Miners' Federation extinguished without a fight in the Nottinghamshire coal-field. There were men of such calibre throughout the county prepared to accept the challenge and continue the struggle while humanly possible. The first step was to ensure the survival of the old Union. There were no facilities for collecting on the pit premises. This now was the prerogative of the new Union. Contact with the men was difficult. Most of the Lodge officials were no longer working at the pit. In this situation there had to be improvisation, and new methods for collecting contributions had to be employed; otherwise the old Union would have succumbed to the machinations of the coal owners and the Spencer Union.

This unique situation had to be faced with unusual methods. It was disappointing, frustrating, even embarrassing, not to be able to collect the contributions on the pit premises. This had been the practice for many years, indeed since the inception of the Union. With a few exceptions the embargo was operating throughout the county coal-field. It seemed like putting the clock back to the days of the Tolpuddle martyrs and the early pioneers of Trade Unionism. Any attempt to collect the contributions on the colliery premises would have meant invoking the law of trespass. The coal owners were in no mood to forego even that. With this embargo operating the full-time officials of the Union, with the consent of the Nottinghamshire Miners' Council, devised a scheme for the appointment of collectors who had to stand on the public highway as near to the colliery premises as possible without being guilty of trespass. Also there had to be door-to-door canvasses and collection. The appointed collectors were like insurance collectors: 'The men from the Pru'.

At the inception of the scheme the T.U.C. agreed to pay eight collectors for three days a week. This was a gesture to help the Union financially. Since the liquid assets of the Nottinghamshire Miners' Association were negligible, the offer was financially more than welcome. Of course, to cover the forty pits in the county it was a small contribution, but in addition to the financial help it meant an identification of the wider Trade Union movement with the struggle in the Nottinghamshire coal-field to preserve free Trade Unionism. All the collectors appointed throughout the county were Lodge officials, in the main unable to obtain work because of their activities during the stoppage. This collective effort, covering almost every pit in the county and maintaining contacts with the men at the pits, did as much as anything to save the Union from extinction.

I was still the secretary of the Sherwood Lodge, and was asked by Mr William Carter, one of the full-time county officials of the Union, to carry on and undertake the job of collector for three days a week. Mr Carter was a fine man, with a good record in the Miners' Union, and was thought highly of by the miners for his sincerity and loyalty to the Union and to the political Labour movement. At the 1918 Parliamentary election, he was the candidate for the Mansfield constituency and was Member of Parliament until 1923. He was like George Spencer, a sponsored miners' candidate, and they entered the House of Commons together. I knew him very well and had a lot to do with him during these dark days, and I know he was pained and wounded in spirit when his colleague, George Spencer, acted as he did. He said to me often that this was an act of betrayal by a man who owed so much to the miners and the Union, and that he should have known better.

At the time of Mr Carter's offer there was no prospect of a job; the offer of ten shillings per day, for three days a week, was, however, something, together with unemployment benefit for the other three days. Also I was in no mood to compromise. Bona fide free Trade Unionism was at stake. I felt an urge to go on, irrespective of what it meant. I shrank from the idea of forsaking my ideals and leaving the Miners' Federation at the time when its fortunes were at its lowest ebb. It was a time when jobs were difficult to obtain, even outside the mining industry. Working at the pit had been the only job I had done since leaving school, and this limited the scope; moreover I was now thirty-one years old. Mr Carter's proposal that I take on the job of collector meant retaining my links and association with the Union. Naturally I discussed the whole matter with my wife, who at no time had complained but had endured the sacrifices with fortitude and courage. We had a four-year-old son, and this naturally came into our calculations and reasoning. To my relief and delight, she said we would go on together and do what we could to restore the fortunes of the Union, and, as a practical demonstration, she went out to do domestic work to help with the family income. It was a courageous decision on her part, and I have always been grateful to her for the part she played and the help and co-operation she gave me.

This system of collecting, and the embargo of the coal owners, continued for eleven years. By no stretch of the imagination was it easy for me and my family, but it was difficult for everybody in the industry. Also the depression of the late 1920s and early 1930s was felt by the workers in all industries throughout the nation. So far as organization was concerned in the Nottinghamshire Miners' Union this period was a difficult one with many ups and down, and so many hopes and disappointments. The constant nagging thought was: 'How long will this situation of two unions—the coal owners' embargo—go on? How will it all end?' The circumstances were most depressing. Some day there would have to be a solution, but no one knew what it would be. Many of us hoped for, and believed in, the final triumph of the Miners' Federation and the elimination of the Spencer Union, and to this end all our thoughts were geared, and with hope and confidence we struggled on.

Standing on the public highway, adjacent to the entrance of the pit premises, in all kinds of weather, collecting the contributions, was no picnic. The reception was mixed. Many of the men went by, uninterested, apathetic, and with no disposition to contribute, looking sideways, and pleased when they had passed. I felt many had a twinge of conscience, for at least by far the majority were good Union men, but of course there was hesitation, because the men feared being seen paying their contribution, and word of this getting back to the management.

There were occasions when there would be an influx to join the Union. Some event would take place, maybe a meeting, a campaign of leaflet distribution, or the emergence of a pit problem which caused dissatisfaction. Then men would come along and say, 'I am going to renew my membership. This situation is intolerable. The longer we stay divided, we shall not get anywhere. Make me a card out!'

The ups and down of the Union were characteristic of this period. The number of men coming back to the Union was most heartening and a tonic to what was sometimes a depressing spirit. Then there would be a falling away. You could not understand or explain it, even to your own satisfaction. It was a mercurial situation; one week or month you were on the mountain top because membership had increased; the next in the valley of despondency, for there had been a falling away. It required the wisdom of Solomon to satisfy yourself or give an adequate reason for the fluctuations; it was a nightmare. However, in spite of the difficulties and fluctuations, an average membership of four to five hundred was maintained at the Sherwood Lodge. This figure was only a third to a quarter of the men employed at the pit. The consolation was that at no time during the eleven years prior to the amalgamation of the two Unions was contact lost. The flag of the Miners' Federation was kept flying!

One item of information that came to my notice in a personal letter to me in 1969, a lapse of over forty years, indicates the extent the screw was tightened so far as the Federation was concerned. The person who wrote me was employed in 1926 at Sherwood as an underground official. We were always great friends who had much in common, particularly in the sphere of books, and our conversations were mutually enjoyed. At no time when I was collecting contributions on the public highway and he was passing would he not stop to talk. Some men would have been embarrassed, and hesitate to pay their contribution in the presence of an official but he was highly respected, and was *persona grata* with all the men. They had no worries. He would not have carried tales to the management about their being members of the Miners' Federation. In his letter, after offering his congratulations upon my becoming a Life Peer, he went on to say, 'What a far cry from 1926! Someone saw me speaking to you at the pit gate when you were not allowed on the premises, and reported it, and for this I was put on the carpet. The General Manager told me that he had heard of senior officials hob-nobbing with communists. When I realized what he meant, I told him that I would not allow anyone to choose my friends, and the day would come when he would be pleased to see you.' Forty-three years passed before I knew this. It reveals how the bitterness of those days extended even to ostracism. Not content with depriving a person of work, and not allowing him on the premises to collect the men's contributions—these were bad enough, but to seek to deprive a man of a friendly conversation was mean, and the equivalent of treating him as a social outcast. In the early post-war period the same General Manager's son was working for the Allied Coal Commission in Germany, and met with a fatal accident; I was now a Member of Parliament and I wrote to his father to offer my sympathy, to which he replied in generous terms. I was happy that the bitterness and hostility of almost twenty years before had evaporated.

Visiting the homes of the men to collect their contributions was an education to me, providing opportunities for discussing the problems of the industry, and reviving nostalgic memories of the stoppage. The best and safest places for the men to talk was in the privacy and quietness of their homes where they would talk frankly and unburden themselves. Good Union men they were, and they felt they had been let down by the drift back to work. One house brings back memories; the father had two sons working at Sherwood. He himself worked at Shirebrook in Derbyshire, but I had to call for the sons' contributions. To him to be out of the Union, the Miners' Federation, was a social crime. I had to settle down for half an hour, often longer, and listen to his philosophy of life, which was a fine one. He was more than sixty years of age, and had been through the mill, having spent his working life in the pit. He was a 'rough diamond', scarred physically and mentally after his long experience in the pit. He was twice my age, and I was happy to sit and listen to the unfolding of his experience. To my knowledge he had taken no official part in the Union, but had been one of the many unknown stalwarts who in sunshine and shadow had 'made' the Miners' Federation. He would talk politics and Trade Unionism. I remember his saying time and again: 'Unity is our strength. Only on this basis can we hope to advance.' At the end of every conversation he would say, 'Bernard, my boy, so glad to see you! Carry on. We shall ultimately triumph. While this situation continues, please call. These lads of mine must never be out of the Union, the Miners' Federation.' Then would come the parting shot, 'What I would do with the coal owners and the

Spencer Union would be to burn them!' From him I learned so much, and got so much encouragement: it was a refreshing weekly experience.

Two others, Abner Holt and Bob Buck, both many years my senior, said little in public, but I remember them clearly for their wisdom, and good sense and loyalty to the Federation. I recall a little while before Bob died, in the early 1950s, persuading him to have a journey by car into the countryside. We went into Clumber Park, through Lime Tree Avenue, calling at the Normanton Inn for refreshments. It was mutually enjoyable relating experiences. Great men they were! It was not long after this meeting that Bob died. Abner had died years before.

In fairness to the management at Sherwood Colliery I must say that although there was persuasion by officials at the pit to join the Spencer Union and attempts to prevent the Nottinghamshire Miners' Association from entering the premises, at no time did they make employment a condition of membership of the Spencer Union as was the practice of some of the companies. But the denial of negotiating on behalf of the members of the Nottinghamshire Miners and the granting of all the pre-stoppage facilities to the Spencer Union made our task of organizing extremely difficult.

At no time was I able to discover the actual membership of the Spencer Union at Sherwood pit, any more than in the county as a whole. Varying figures were bandied about but it was impossible to ascertain the exact membership or the effective extent of their deliberations with the management. I knew the men cursed about the latter.

The gulf between the two sides was so wide, county- and pit-wise, that they were not on speaking terms, and relationships were sour and bitter. The circumstances of bitterness at the pit, at the pub, in the home even, had to be witnessed to be believed. Some of the men were in one Union, some in the others, and many outside either of the two. Cohesion and unity had gone. The men who contributed to the Nottinghamshire Miners' Association, did so out of sheer loyalty and hope for its ultimate triumph, though there was so little it could offer. It was regrettable and a great disadvantage to the representatives of the Nottinghamshire Miners' Association that its members were deprived of negotiating opportunities so that they were unable to take up with the management the men's grievances and problems. Men cursed, in unprintable language, but it was of no avail. The coal owners and the management in the Nottinghamshire coal-field rejoiced that the men were divided.

There was one matter and only one in which the Nottinghamshire Miners' Association could do anything for the men, and this was in the sphere of Workmen's Compensation. This was not unimportant because in coal-mining, where the incidence of accident and industrial disease was high, there were always disputes about payment under the Workmen's Compensation Acts. In Nottinghamshire the position was that some of the companies had joined together to form the Midland Coalowners' Indemnity Company. The Sherwood Company and others farmed out their liabilities to private insurance companies. A firm in Nottingham, P. F. Scanlon, was the insurer for the Sherwood Company. This meant that in the case of a dispute either for total or partial compensation the management did not come into the matter at all. All the negotiations were with the insurance company. There were many problems and grievances in this particular field: 'Did the accident arise out of, and in the course of, employment? Was the accident reported?' These were statutory requirements. There was also the matter of men partially recovered but unable to go back to their pre-accident occupation and yet medically certified as fit for light work. This was always a tricky business and usually meant protracted negotiations, often ending with a medical referee or the County Court judge for a decision. Again, industrial diseases like miners' nystagmus, dermatitis, beat knee and beat elbow were difficult matters. The partially recovered man, unable to resume his normal occupation might or might not be given lighter work. There was no legal obligation for the employer to do this. If he did, the remuneration would be less, and the legal formula upon which compensation was based worked in this way: the miner was entitled to half the difference between his pre-accident twelve monthly average earnings and what he would actually receive post-accident or what he was able to earn, even if no light job was available, up to a maximum payment of thirty shillings per week (even for total disability this was the figure). There was little trouble with regard to total disability once the claim for such was established, but so often there was difficulty when the man was partially recovered. Once the extent of the man's ability to work was agreed, his compensation payment would be arrived at in the following way: If the man's pre-accident twelve monthly earnings were fifty shillings a week, and the post-accident amount he was actually earning with a job or able to earn was forty shillings a week (presuming the employer was unable or unwilling to employ him) the partial compensation (or half difference as it was called in mining areas) would be five shillings a week. In the days of the late 1920s and the 1930s fifty shillings was liberal for the average miner's wage in the Nottinghamshire and Derbyshire coal-fields. In 1930 it was forty-five shillings a week, and this average figure obscures the fact that whilst some of the miners could be receiving more, large numbers would be receiving less. To my personal knowledge there were many men who, because of low pre-accident earnings, were not entitled legally to any partial compensation at all, however severe their disability might be.

Not all the disabled men were given jobs. There was no legal liability for the employer to do this—though some were more generous than others. The management at Sherwood pit had a good record and were as good as the best in finding disabled men jobs, but many disabled miners in the 1930s had a raw deal. These men were doubly unfortunate: firstly to be victims of accident or recognized industrial disease, and secondly that it happened at a time when wages were low, and days worked per week few. These circumstances affected not only their earnings, but also their compensation. The negotiations for settling a claim in case of dispute for either full or partial compensation for men at Sherwood pit were between the Union and the insurance company. The matter of employment for a partially recovered man was for the management of the colliery. At this point the Nottinghamshire Miners' Association was at a disadvantage because of the rigidly kept embargo; there was no equivocation and the negotiations on any matter were entirely in the hands of the Spencer Union. Unable to approach the management in an effort to obtain a job for a disabled man who was one of our members, we had to suggest to the man that he approach the manager himself for lighter work. This was when the embargo on the Nottinghamshire Miners' Association prevented any other action. We were entirely dependent upon the loyalty of the men, and their faith in preserving the old Union, as to whether they continued their membership. We could only hope that one day the Union would triumph over the combined forces of the coal owners and the Spencer Union. All praise to the men at Sherwood and the thousands throughout the county in those far-off days, who in spite of the fact we could do so little for them, never wavered in their loyalty to the Miners' Federation and the cause of free Trade Unionism.

In addition to the work as a collector and secretary of the Sherwood Lodge, I was addressing meetings with the full-time officials, particularly in and around Mansfield. One of the officials, Frank Varley, M.P. for the Mansfield division, was a sick man and lived for only three years after the setting up of the Spencer Union. In addition to being Member of Parliament, he was the Nottinghamshire member of the National Executive of the Miners' Federation and had been since before the stoppage of 1926. He had been subject to criticism during the stoppage for outlining proposals for a settlement in a weekly paper the *New Leader*. The criticism of him was that, before rushing into print, as a member of the National Executive, he should have brought the proposals before the Executive Committee to find out their reactions. His stand against the Spencer Union was short-lived for he died on 17 March 1929.

Wherever there was hope of reviving a Branch of the Union or restarting one where it had lapsed, a meeting was called. It was not always easy to organize. A number of them would be in the open air, some in a public house. Sometimes there would be a good response, at other times there was no response at all. It took some understanding, but there could be no doubt as to the changed circumstances since 1926. For those responsible for the meetings there was a mixture of hope and despondency. Wages were getting lower, unemployment was rising and grievances were multiplying. The owners were riding high and they knew that they could impose almost anything on the men, for there was no effective challenge to anything. Bitterness and suspicion between the men of the two Unions had to be witnessed to be believed. Families were estranged, and there were even households where different members belonged to different Unions.

The Nottinghamshire coal-field in the late 1920s and early 1930s was a shambles. Particularly in the remote exclusive mining villages, the area was a prison or a fortress from which there was not the slightest chance of escape. I still doubt whether the magnitude of repression, intolerance and bitterness was fully appreciated amongst those outside the Nottinghamshire coal-field. Those of us living amongst it, and actively engaged in the struggle against Company Unionism, often wondered whether the other county unions of the Federation, or the Miners' Federation, or the wider Trade Union movement, really fully appreciated the conditions prevailing at that time in the Nottinghamshire coal-field. You really had to be living amongst it to grasp the full significance of the bitterness that existed.

In the newly created exclusive mining communities such as Blidworth, Bilsthorpe, Clipstone, Welbeck, Edwinstowe, Ollerton, and Harworth, where the most recent and largest pits were, houses for the miners had been built quite near to the pits; in fact almost everything was the property of the colliery companies. The landlords from whom the land had been purchased were going to benefit financially from coal royalties. From rural villages they had, with the sinking of pits, been transformed into mining communities, though somewhat remote and isolated. Penetration and propaganda in the late 1920s and 1930s were difficult in these places; communications were not easy; the villages were off the beaten track and 'bus services were not good.

At some of these pits every encouragement was given to the Spencer Union; at some, employment was conditional upon membership of the Spencer Union. It was difficult for these men, and the choice was not only a job, but the house too. They were tied cottages; if your job went your house went too. In these places particularly the task of reorganizing and rebuilding the Nottinghamshire Miners' Union and saving the Lodge was not easy. It was almost impossible and the marvel is that the organization survived, but survive it did. The faithful souls in these places were responsible for the survival of the Association and deserve the credit.

In Bilsthorpe, the Todhunter family, migrants from the Durham coal-field, at Blidworth the late Bob Jones, and other worthy men at Bilsthorpe, Welbeck, Edwinstowe and Clipstone, kept the Union alive. One particular memory among many remains. Mr Carter asked if I would go to Blidworth, where, he said, there was a spontaneous outburst of feeling against the Spencer Union and the attitude of the management. Leaflets announcing the date and place of the meeting were distributed. We met at the 'Black Bull' public house in the old village. It was well away from the colliery premises, and apart from the open air, it was the only place we could meet. What a meeting it was, and a unanimous condemnation of the Spencer Union was given by the two to three hundred men there! I thought this a real achievement, and the spirit surprised me and gave me great pleasure.

The men made a united demand for restarting a branch of the Nottinghamshire Miners' Association, which we did. Scores of men paid contributions and took cards, and the next step was the appointment of a Secretary. The normal practice was for the Secretary to be employed at the pit, but there were fears of repercussions in the form of the 'sack' if anyone employed at the pit became Secretary, and this would also have meant the loss of his house. So I was asked to act as Secretary, and every Sunday morning I went to collect the contributions hoping that this would last for a short time only.

For some time the Branch thrived and the meetings were well attended. Confidence gradually grew from this new beginning at Blidworth. But eventually the pit closed. It was said that geological conditions had become so poor that the pit was not an economic proposition. But whether this was the real reason I do not know. There was no consultation at that

time as there is now, and of course had this been so it would
not have been with the representatives of the Nottinghamshire
Miners' Association officials, who were anathema to the coal
owners. A number of years afterwards the pit was reopened
and at the time of writing is still in production. The closure
was a terrible blow to the Blidworth community. Some of the
men obtained jobs, others were unemployed. I recall members
of this pit with admiration and pleasure, particularly the late
Bob Jones, Ron Self, and also the Crewe family, and Sam
Kilbey and his wife, the Lingard family, Harry Stacey and
Cyril Schofield.

In 1929 the concern of the Miners' Federation over the
situation in the Nottinghamshire coal-field was growing and
the Trades' Union Congress were apprehensive about this
challenge to free Trade Unionism. It was decided to have a
ballot of the whole coal-field to ascertain from the men which
Union they preferred, the Nottinghamshire Miners' Association or the Spencer Union. At the request of the Miners'
Federation, the T.U.C. came into the picture and undertook
to be responsible for and to organize the ballot. This was as
good as a tonic to many of us. Our seeming isolation was to
be broken, and we were not being forgotten by the wider
movement in the struggle to resuscitate free Trade Unionism
in the coal-field. Before taking the ballot, a sub-committee of
the T.U.C. met the Nottinghamshire coal owners in March
1929. It was an endeavour to stop the discrimination of the
coal owners in favour of the Spencer Union. What a hope it
was! Nevertheless the effort was heartening. The owners denied
discrimination. To the miners in the county the denial was
moonshine. The owners did agree to issue a public statement,
and this was given wide publicity by the Trades' Union Congress. The statement was as follows: 'The Nottinghamshire
coal owners intend loyally to carry out the agreement made
with the representatives of their workmen (the Spencer Union)
and cannot recognize any other organization than that with
which they are now dealing. The Nottinghamshire Coalowners' Association, however, make no enquiry or discrimination in regard to a man's Trade Union.' The latter part of
this statement convinced no one and was the negation of what

was being practised at many of the Nottinghamshire pits, sometimes positively, at others in a more passive manner. Those who were living with it every day, and especially those who were the victims, knew the statement to be false.

The ballot took place on 30 April 1929, one month after the T.U.C. had met the owners. It was preceded by a speaking campaign throughout the coal-field. The organizing of the ballot was in the hands of the assistant secretary of the T.U.C., Mr Vincent Tewson, now Sir Vincent. He spent some time at the headquarters of the Nottinghamshire Miners' Association organizing and directing the event. It was a difficult undertaking. There were physical hurdles to surmount. There was no access to the colliery premises and at many of the pits, if not all, the ballot was taken on the public highway. Not even the T.U.C. was allowed to use the pit-yard. The owners were not interested in free democratic expression to resolve the difficulty. They obviously were fully satisfied with the prevailing disunity which suited them. After all, the situation was partly their creation. There were no pressures or threats by the T.U.C. They wanted a free expression of opinion as to what the men wanted. At the meetings there was advocacy of the case and cause of the Nottinghamshire Miners' Association and the Federation. It was for the men to make up their own minds, and to take advantage of the opportunity to say which Union they wanted. Of course it was boycotted by the Spencer Union. This was expected and gave no surprise. The owners in their ivory tower were not interested let alone perturbed. They knew that whatever the result, it did not matter, for they were the masters and would have the last word. And so they did!

The ballot was generally supervised by a reputable firm of Nottingham solicitors, and every endeavour was made to ensure that the votes were properly taken and counted. In spite of the physical difficulties, there had been a good numerical response, and there was a resounding victory for the Nottinghamshire Miners' Association! 32,277 had voted for the old union and 2,533 for the Spencer Union. As anticipated it made no difference to the attitude of the coal owners. In fact, like Pharaoh, their hearts hardened, and victimization continued at some pits towards men who were active in the Nottinghamshire Miners' Association. It was not the end of the road yet. The coal owners with economic power in their hands were unmoved by the result of the ballot. A free, democratic expression meant nought to them: it was their industry. They would run it and organize it just as they wished. They would negotiate with whom they decided. There was liberal use of that economic weapon, 'the sack', towards anyone who was prepared to stand up for what the ballot had revealed: 'The right to choose which Union the men desired'. The coal owners were adamant and immovable. Like the rock of Gibraltar they stood firm against all comers: the Nottinghamshire Miners' Association, the Miners' Federation, even the T.U.C. The Spencer Union, too, took no notice, for the ballot meant nothing at all to them. The men in the coal-field knew what they wanted and had so voted, but it seemed that there was no way to implement their view. A strike was out of the question at this time. The men were licking their wounds after the defeat of 1926, cursing the coal owners and the Spencer Union, and were in the slough of despondency. The fire of enthusiasm so predominant in 1926 appeared to have burnt out. It was the hope and belief of many that it would be rekindled, but when? It was obvious the time was not at that moment, but, come it would one day, some of us had no doubt! In 1929 the ballot was over and there was no visible sign of any change. It was like looking into a tunnel, so long, without visible light. How long, oh Lord? was inwardly felt if not expressed.

The months rolled on and became years. The same routine of collecting, canvassing, addressing and attending meetings went on, but we were impotent to do anything effectively to achieve recognition of the Union and this was so important. As well as being Secretary of the Sherwood Lodge, I took on the duties of delegate to the Miners' Council. This dual holding of office would have been unthinkable in normal circumstances and contrary to the rules of the Association. The view was expressed in the Lodge meetings that I was free, with no possibility of repercussions from the management, and the best course under the circumstances was for me to attend the monthly meetings at the Union's headquarters, at Basford in Nottingham. I was collector, Secretary and Delegate. Many in the county had no jobs at the pit but were anxious to preserve the identity of the Nottinghamshire Miners' Association—a very difficult task. There were grumblings in every part of the coal-field and it was obvious that feelings of resentment were growing stronger. Sometime, somewhere in the county we believed those feelings would erupt, but where and when, and how it would end was anybody's guess. Would it be by fusion of the two Unions which was being talked about, or a fight to the finish? In many quarters the idea of fusion was resented; in some circles it was believed to be the only way to resolve the problem. I, personally, along with others nationally and locally, was opposed to the idea. I thought it wrong, after all that had happened, and the manner in which the majority of the men had expressed their feelings.

In this position of stalemate the hope was that the feeling of discontent of the men would, at some stage, some time, somewhere, make them revolt at being denied their freedom of choice. It was only a hope, and a hope for a long time deferred. It did eventually happen, however, and when it did it was marked with bitterness and intolerance and resulted in desperate hardship and sacrifice by the thousands of miners in the county.

CHAPTER VII

Harworth

The Harworth Colliery, owned by the Barber-Walker Company, was in an old-world village in the extreme north of Nottinghamshire quite near the Yorkshire border. The company had extensive interests in coal in the Eastwood area of Nottinghamshire, and had carried on mining operations for many years. The mining area of Eastwood has become well known through the writings of D. H. Lawrence who was born and lived there, and whose family was employed at one of the Barber-Walker pits. The Company also were the owners of the Bentley Colliery near Doncaster in the South Yorkshire coal-field. Adjacent to the Harworth Colliery an entirely new village had been built; it was well planned and had new modern houses to accommodate the influx of miners who had obtained work at the pit. The name given to this new mining village was Bircotes. The pit still retains the name of Harworth, but the village where the miners live is always referred to as Bircotes.

All the land and property in this new village as distinct from Harworth, belonged to the Colliery Company, except one plot of land which belonged to the Doncaster Co-operative Society. This was in the 1920s and 1930s, forty years ago. It was thirty-five miles from Nottingham (where the Nottinghamshire Miners' headquarters were situated), eight miles from Doncaster, and a similar distance from Worksop. It was a new community of miners isolated and remote; numbers of men had migrated from the Durham coal-field, and with their families had settled in this new village of Bircotes to work at the Harworth pit. Often I have heard Pembrokeshire referred to as 'little England beyond Wales'. The description of

'Durham in Notts' could rightly be ascribed to Harworth pit and Bircotes village.

The Geordies, numerous, and speaking in their northern dialect, were steeped in Trade Unionism, proud of their Durham Miners' Association, their native county and their heritage. In July of every year many of them made the journey to attend the Durham Miners' Big Meeting as it was called and is still spoken of, and would on no account miss it. What Mecca means to the Mohammedans, the Durham 'Big Meeting' meant to these Durham miners in Harworth. There were also Yorkshire, Nottinghamshire and Derbyshire miners who had migrated to Harworth, but the preponderance of the Geordies was evident.

Following the lock-out of 1926, organization here was difficult. The embargo of the Nottinghamshire coal owners, the remoteness of the place and the distance from the headquarters of the Union, were factors militating against organization. The South Yorkshire coal-field, including Maltby and Firbeck pits, was only a short distance away and this meant that the pits around Doncaster were nearer to Harworth than some of the Nottinghamshire pits. The embargo by the Nottinghamshire coal owners and their attitude to the Nottinghamshire Miners' Association were not prevalent in the Yorkshire coal-field. Organization after the lock-out would have been more effective if made by the Yorkshire Miners' Association. My information is that there were only seven members of the Nottinghamshire Miners' Association in 1935 at Harworth. In spite of this, it was here at Harworth that the discontent prevalent throughout the Nottinghamshire coal-field erupted.

One day in 1933 I had a surprise visitor at my home, a person of whom I had not hitherto heard, a complete stranger who had made the journey from London. He had been to the Miners' offices in Nottingham, and the officials suggested he should call on me to help and advise him in his mission; he had their permission and blessing to write about and expose the conditions in the Nottinghamshire coal-field. He was a journalist and had been engaged by Reynolds Sunday newspaper to visit the Nottinghamshire coal-field, and especially

66

Harworth, and write an article. It was late in the afternoon
when he arrived at my home. He explained the purpose of his
visit, and asked if he could get to Harworth that day and if
I would accompany him. Harworth was twenty miles away;
there was an infrequent, inconvenient bus service that made it
impossible to get back to Mansfield Woodhouse that day. My
wife and I asked him to stay the night. I recall saying to him,
'Where there is heart room, there is hearth room'. He said
he would like to stay but insisted he go to the shop for some
groceries. We did not like the idea, but away to the shop he
went. I accompanied him, and we returned with the goods he
had bought. The next day I arranged with a friend of mine
who had a baby-Austin car to take us to Harworth.

When we arrived at Harworth we went to the 'Galway
Arms'. We had no contacts for we knew no one and found
little disposition to talk from those whom we did approach. It
was my first visit to Harworth and the last of my thoughts was
that I should, one day, witness a struggle there to re-establish
the right for a miner to join the Union of his choice. The
journalist was amazed at what he heard, and from men who
were not too inclined to unburden themselves.

The article appeared in *Reynolds News* in January 1933. I
have it before me as I write. It was headlined in big black
type which in some small measure will convey what was
happening in the Nottinghamshire coal-field at the time:
'Mussolini methods in the Coal-field', 'Pitmen victimised for
loyalty to their fellows', 'Nottingham reign of Terror'. The
closing paragraph of the article was as follows: 'As I shook
hands with miner friends, I asked myself: "Was I really in
the Britain of 1932?" It seemed almost impossible.' The man
who visited Harworth and other parts of the County was Mr
George Bilainkin, a diplomatic journalist and writer of many
books on the Far East. After nearly forty years, I recently met
him and he recalls his visit to Harworth very clearly.

Another four years passed from the visit of Mr Bilainkin to
the beginning of the eruption at Harworth. 'Dirt deductions'
from the men's output and general dissatisfaction with conditions at the pit lit the fuse. Patience was exhausted, and the
end of the road of no negotiations with the Nottinghamshire

Miners' Association and no recognition of the Miners' Federation had been reached. The Lodge of the Nottinghamshire Miners was resuscitated. Mick Kane became President of the Lodge and Ephraim Patchett, Delegate, David Buckley, Secretary, and Frank Holmes, Treasurer, with a small committee.

This was a real achievement. The grievances and dissatisfaction then reached boiling point and the President and Delegate were chosen to seek an interview with the manager to discuss the grievances. A blank refusal was the answer because the Nottinghamshire Miners' Association, whom the delegation were representing, was not recognized by the Company—the same story as at every other Nottinghamshire pit. (See Appendices A to D). There was still this obdurate, unrelenting, attitude by the coal owners towards the Nottinghamshire Miners' Association. Even after ten years it was either the Spencer Union or no negotiations, so far as the owners were concerned.

Between August and November of 1936 the complaints at Harworth did not become fewer, nor did the management relent. The question of dirt deductions, which were affecting the wage packet of the piece-rate workers, the coal-getters, had become a running sore. Ventilation on one of the districts was causing concern. Also there was an allegation that an under-official—a deputy—had struck two boys. Notice given to four men to terminate their employment did not improve matters. There was a combination of grievances confined to the pit which could have been settled but were not because attempts to meet the manager to discuss the grievances failed. He would not listen to the men. They were in and out on strike. The problem of dirt deduction was as follows : instead of the coal-getters being paid the total weight of what was in the tubs as they came out of the pit and over the weighing machine, there was a percentage deduction for dirt, a percentage the men thought excessive. There were also difficulties and dissatisfaction with the check-weighmen over this.

The men held a meeting in the pit-yard about the question of dirt deductions on 16 November 1936. There was no satisfaction forthcoming, for the management still refused to meet a deputation, so the following day the majority of the men struck. Their attitude was 'Enough is Enough'. It turned out to be the beginning of a long struggle and the opening of an important chapter in Trade Union history.

As it progressed, the Miners' Federation became directly involved and the Government too. After months of struggle, in some way, by some means, the problem in the Nottinghamshire coal-field had to be resolved. On the first day of the stoppage, 17 November, the Company announced that the men who had struck were no longer in their employ. Legally, it is true the men had broken their contract, but they were desperate and desperation reaches a point when men are not concerned with legal niceties. In effect, they were saying 'to hell' with the Company's embargo and the Spencer Union— 'We are men, and have a right to be able to ventilate and discuss our grievances.' For two months they had been trying to meet the management over their grievances. The representatives of the Spencer Union would not, or at any rate did not, seek to resolve the problems, and every time the men, as representatives of the Nottinghamshire Miners' Association, applied for an interview, the answer was 'no'.

The last straw came on 19 November, the third day of the strike. Instructions were given by the management that, on return to work, each man would sign a declaration that he was willing to become a member of the Spencer Union. Three weeks before this ultimatum, a ballot had been taken to ascertain which Union the men wanted to represent them. There was an overwhelming majority in favour of the Nottinghamshire Miners' Association: 1,175 to 145. This, like the county coal-field ballot seven years earlier, had no effect on the management at Harworth pit. They dug their toes in, hardened their hearts, and not only refused to meet the representatives of the Nottinghamshire Miners' Association, but stated that not one man would work there unless he became a member of the Spencer Union. Loss of job meant loss of house too but the threat of this double penalty did not deter or frighten the men.

The stage was now set. Local grievances receded into the background and the real issue was joined, which was recognition of the Nottinghamshire Miners' Association, a part of the Miners' Federation. Authority for this was given when the Miners' Federation made the strike official and undertook the responsibility through the Nottinghamshire Miners' Association of giving all help possible. The struggle of the Harworth men was the struggle of the Federation until the Nottinghamshire problem was resolved. I said at the time and I have not changed my opinion since : the Harworth dispute ranks in first importance with any episode in British Trade Union history, since the days of the Dorchester Labourers who became famous as the Tolpuddle Martyrs. 1936 was a landmark, indicating that men are neither willing nor prepared to suffer repression for ever, and to be denied the right of choosing their own organization. A thing imposed because the other fellow is stronger than you is only transient. It is only a question of time before revolt will come. So it was in the Nottinghamshire coal-field.

With mounting discontent, the explosion of resentment happened in the place least thought of, Harworth. Ten wearying, uncertain years had passed since the end of the stoppage and the beginning of the rival Union. In December 1936, I was asked by Mr Val Coleman, the General Secretary of the Nottinghamshire Miners' Association on behalf of the Executive, to go out to Harworth, live there, and act as the Union's representative. He had arranged accommodation for me with Mr Frank Holmes, treasurer of the newly-formed Branch. I agreed, and from Sunday to Thursday of every week while the dispute was on, I remained in Harworth, assisting in every possible way in collaboration with the Lodge Committee : addressing meetings and receiving information from the Union's headquarters to transmit eagerly awaited news to the men. I had to return for the Friday to take my place at Sherwood to collect the contributions, visit the homes of the members for their contributions and attend to any Lodge business.

I would like to pay a tribute to Frank Holmes and his wife for their great kindness to me, and their unswerving loyalty to the Miners' Federation. In the end Frank did not resume work at Harworth, but at the end of the stoppage he secured employment at Maltby pit in South Yorkshire, where he remained until his retirement. In 1969 at the age of eighty, he died. We remained good, firm friends up to his death and I attended his funeral. It was the breaking of a link in a friendship of thirty-two years—a friendship born in struggle.

There were many other good and loyal people with whom I formed a friendship then : the Slater family; Archie, the son, was a tower of strength at any hour, always at the ready with his car to do any job. There were Mick Kane, Ephraim Patchett, and Bob Brown, who went to Spain during the Civil War; Bill Wainwright, Dave Buckley, Secretary of the Lodge, Jack Smith and a host of others, the majority from the Durham coal-field. I have always been loud and forthcoming in my praise of the men and women of Harworth in 1936 and 1937. Many have died. Their memory I revere. To have known them was a privilege and I shall always remember their loyalty and devotion, and the part they played in striking a blow for free Trade Unionism, and their resentment against the repressive attitude and measures of their employers.

Many police were drafted into the village—how many I do not know, but they were everywhere. I arrived in Harworth in early December 1936, and was introduced to the Lodge officials. One incident I remember well : one late afternoon in company with two of the Lodge officials, we walked round the village. It was advisable not to go alone in case something happened ; the evidence of more than one was important. We had not been walking for long when a group of men told us the news that two men had been arrested and taken to the police station. Losing no time, we hastened to the police station. When we arrived, we saw a crowd of a few hundred men and women who were very angry that two of the strikers were inside and were determined to get them out. They were lined up in front of the police station. The police were there too in considerable numbers, and their batons were drawn. It was an ugly, menacing scene. I made my way to the front of the crowd to speak to the Superintendent ; he was not at all responsive, and regarded my approach to him as an intrusion. I was anxious to avoid trouble and prevent any physical violence, which I had a feeling could happen as so many police were there with batons drawn. He too must have thought that something could happen. Not pleasantly, he asked me who I was. I told him that the Union had sent me out to Harworth to be of any assistance possible in the conduct of the dispute. I was there in a representative capacity. 'How do I know who you are?' he asked again, aggressively. With every passing moment I felt time was running out and wondered if this was to be the first clash between the strikers and the police. Anxious to avoid trouble and in desperation, I said to the Superintendent, 'In answer to your question "Who are you?"—I could say "I am one of a number regarded as your employers".' I further told him I was a member of the Nottinghamshire County Council, which body is responsible for the administration of the County Police. I thought he was sceptical about this and to remove any doubt about it, I showed him my name and the area I represented in the year book of the County Council. He was still reluctant to allow me to talk to him about the situation and the possibility of averting a clash which could result in a building being wrecked, and people being hurt.

But I think the conversation restrained the impatience of the men and women. At last he relented and said he would see me privately. Immediately I jumped on to a wall and asked the crowd to follow me to the only plot of vacant land that was not the property of the Colliery Company. When they assembled I told them that the Superintendent had consented to an interview and we would all meet again in the Market Hall at 7.30 p.m. when I would report. There was no doubt that a serious incident was averted.

The outcome was that the two men were charged and then released. Eventually they were summoned to appear at the Worksop Police Court where they were fined. These were the first summonses of many to follow. I do not know how many summonses there were during the next six months but there were at least some men every week from Harworth who had to appear before the magistrate in the Worksop Court on charges arising out of the dispute. In the initial stages the penalties were fines, but worse was to follow in the form of imprisonment.

There were some men who continued to work—the number

was not known. The pit remained open but the output of coal was negligible, barely sufficient for internal consumption at the pit. It kept the plant in order and little more. But of course the fact that some men were working was an irritation to those on strike. Picketing at the pit-gate was employed; there was also an innovation to show the displeasure of those on strike towards those continuing to work: every evening, at the time the night shift began, those still at work would assemble at a given spot, the end of Droversdale Road, a distance of at least half a mile from the pit-yard entrance. From this point, with police in front, at the rear and on either side, they marched to the pit-yard. Scrooby Road, which they entered from Droversdale Road, was a long stretch from the main road, a long promenade which ran past the colliery entrance. On this stretch of road every night in the darkness, in all kinds of weather, hundreds of men and women congregated to watch this nightly march, not out of curiosity, but to demonstrate collectively their disapproval towards the 'strike breakers'.

It was called the chain gang. Many of the strikers were apprehended by the police, rushed to the police station and charged and eventually summoned to appear at the Worksop Court. Many of the arrests and summonses were not justified, for apart from vocal disapproval, there was no evidence of physical interference at this nightly happening.

I recall one Sunday evening after a meeting in the picture house at which Edward Dunn, M.P. was the speaker. At my suggestion, the meeting was closed early so that we could see the 'chain gang' procession. If a meeting was going on too long, someone would shout out or the Chairman would be asked, 'What about the chain gang?' This nightly ritual, as it came to be described, had not to be missed. Ted Dunn and I walked together along the promenade, and stood opposite the entrance to the pit-yard. It was a dark evening. Hundreds of people were there, from the meeting, the homes, the church and the pub. A man standing quite close to Mr Dunn and myself was apprehended. It could have been either of us. What a sensation! The headline in the Press would read, 'Member of Parliament and County Councillor arrested at

73

Harworth'. It might have been a good thing! The man, like Ted Dunn and myself was just standing there, looking on, and not even booing as the chain gang went by, yet he was apprehended. I said to Ted, 'That is common practice.' Together we went to the police station where the man was being detained. We spoke to the sergeant in charge. Mr Dunn introduced himself as the Member of Parliament for Rother Valley in the West Riding of Yorkshire. I am sure it was a shock for the sergeant when Mr Dunn protested the man's innocence of untoward behaviour as he was there, an eye witness as to what had taken place. He said that if the man was not released, he would, the following day, report the matter to the Home Secretary and raise the matter in the House of Commons. The man was released and no charge was made.

Christmas of 1936 came; the year 1937 dawned; the spring came and yet there was no sign of the stoppage ending. As the weeks became months, the determination of the men and their women did not abate—bitterness became more pronounced. There was strike pay through the Miners' Federation. Weekly collections were organized, and men and women, every Friday, were taken by bus to the pits in Nottinghamshire and Derbyshire to collect. Of course like the Union collectors in Nottinghamshire they had to stand on the public highway, as they were not allowed on the pit premises. The miners in the two county coal-fields responded generously. Wages were not high, but they felt Harworth was their struggle too. Also a test case was put up before the umpire for unemployment benefit. It was successful and the men eventually received unemployment benefit.

There was plenty of evidence of provocation designed to break the spirit of the men. They knew that the chairman of the Colliery Company was the chairman of the County Council, but it did not matter—there was no sign of weakening, and the will and spirit to go on continued. Resources did not in any way provide luxuries but were sufficient to keep the wolf from the door, and this was a change from 1926. One person, a fish merchant in Grimsby, Ernest Marklew, who at one time was Member of Parliament for Colne Valley in Yorkshire, daily sent a consignment of fish which was distributed by the Committee to those on strike. This was greatly appreciated.

There was no evidence of weakness or relenting on the part of the Company. Their pits in the Eastwood area and the one in Yorkshire were working and it was not possible to predict how long the strike would go on, or what the outcome would be. Their obvious determination to starve the men into submission, so far as one could see, would not succeed. The taking out of summonses was as common as the buttercups growing in the fields. There were many incidents between the men on strike and the police. The longer the strike continued, the more frequent did appearances at the Worksop Court become.

The worst incident of the dispute was one Saturday evening. The weekly dance and social was taking place in the Market Hall. The police went there to deliver summonses to a number of the men; the whole thing flared up, and a running battle began. There were many casualties and much damage to property. I myself was in Mansfield Woodhouse having left the previous day to do my collecting. I returned as usual to Harworth on the Sunday, earlier than usual, having been informed what had taken place the previous evening. I heard the story from the men and listened to evidence of the magnitude of the damage: cars overturned and in the Miners' Institute (a place not frequented during the dispute by the men on strike as this was the property of the Colliery Company) every pane of glass was broken. The Market Hall even on the Sunday, the day after the incident, looked more like a slaughterhouse than a dance hall. Men were bruised, cut and bandaged; indeed it was a sorry and unpleasant sight.

I listened to what the men had to say and I concluded it was a mistake that the police should have gone to the Market Hall that evening to deliver the summonses. This could have been done, as is the usual practice, at the home of each individual person or sent by post. Had this been done, this particularly serious incident would have been averted. It was an ugly happening, and tempers got out of control, and as a consequence there was much damage.

Harworth was now national news. The radio and the press gave prominence to it, and in all the coal-fields it became a talking point and remained so for a long time. Mr Ronald Kidd of the National Council for Civil Liberties came out, took a lot of evidence, and his organization published a report. Ritchie Calder, now a Life Peer, also paid a visit for the *Daily Herald*. We became great friends during his stay in Harworth, and now in the House of Lords we often talk of that meeting, the events there, and our sharing of a room at the home of Mr and Mrs Holmes. A number of men and one woman were charged by the police and summoned to appear before the magistrates at Worksop Court.

Sir Stafford Cripps came to the local court to represent the accused. I went to the proceedings and I remember the magistrate's clerk during the proceedings jumping up and down like a jack-in-the-box, restless, impatient and loquacious. Sir Stafford endured this for some time, but at last he took him to task about his manner. Politely but firmly he told him what his duty was as a servant of the Court. Had I been in the place of the clerk and had there been a mouse hole, I would have made for it!

The final culmination was the appearance of sixteen men and one woman at the Nottinghamshire Assizes, which were held on 23 June. Sir Stafford was unable to appear. The judge was Mr Justice Singleton, and the following were the sentences: Mick Kane, two years' imprisonment; two of fifteen months; one of twelve months; six, including Mrs Haymer, of nine months; one of six months; one of four months and one bound over to keep the peace.

A fund was launched to help the dependents of those who had gone to prison. The patrons were Fred Bellenger, the Member of Parliament for Bassetlaw in which constituency Harworth was, Ted Dunn, M.P., who took a great interest in the Harworth dispute and was always available to give help and advice, and Alderman Harry Hartland, a magistrate of the Worksop Court. The members of the Funds' Committee were Harworth men and women. The appeal was a national one, and the response came from Trade Unions, local Labour Parties, Co-operative Societies, Women's Co-operative Guilds and individuals. The list of subscribers was from all parts of Britain, and the amount subscribed was £1,296 of which £980 was disbursed to the dependents.

Every night of the week during the dispute, except Friday, there were meetings and social gatherings. They had, of course, to terminate in time to watch the chain gang being escorted to the pit. On reflection, the number of hours I spent speaking to the men and women over the six months is staggering. Every imaginable subject was discussed : Trade Unionism, Parliament and National Politics, Local Government, and sometimes we had a 'question and answer' evening. The men and women from the north would sing the folk songs of their native county. They would talk of the struggles of their native Durham and Northumberland, and the part their forebears played in the building of the miners' organization. A lot of its history they had listened to and learnt in their homes during childhood, and they felt and were convinced that they were carrying on the tradition of their fathers to try to establish the right to band together in the Union of their choice. I learnt much from these courageous and proud people.

The Miners' Federation was now involved up to the hilt in the dispute, and was pleased that the opportunity had come in Nottinghamshire to provide a possible breakthrough in order to restore the unity in the coal-field which had been broken since 1926.

From January 1937 to the end of the dispute of the same year, the main preoccupation of the National Executive was the position in Nottinghamshire—Harworth being the centre-piece of the discussions, and there were correspondence and meetings with the Secretary for Mines. At this time the Mines' Department was a part of the Board of Trade, not a separate Ministry as it is now. These discussions were reported to the Nottinghamshire Miners' delegate council meetings and, in this period, the idea of fusion of the two Unions was discussed. There were some members of the Federation who were of the opinion that this was the solution. This was not, however, the feeling of the men at Harworth, nor of a considerable number of men throughout the British coal-field.

Matters in January 1937 were on the boil. On 20 January there was a special delegate conference of the Federation to decide policy on the Harworth dispute (which had been going on from September of the previous year). Some of the leaders were for fusion; others wanted to see the Spencer Union crushed. This division of opinion existed even among the officials in the Nottinghamshire coal-field. Herbert Booth, the President, and William Bayliss, one of the full-time officials since the death of William Carter in 1932, were in opposition on this question. Herbert Booth was for fusion; William Bayliss against. Val. Coleman, General Secretary, was not so outspoken on the issue, but supported Mr Bayliss.

At the conference, a resolution was carried giving authority to the Executive to take a ballot vote of the British coal-field on the question of enforcing the principle of the freedom of organization and Trade Union recognition for those so organized. At the Nottinghamshire Miners' council meeting on 27 January a report was given of a meeting that had taken place with the Federation officials and the proceedings of the Conference. I remember this meeting very well. Herbert Booth found little support for fusion among the delegates to the meeting, and vacated the chair, resigned the Presidency and left the meeting. This was tragic but Herbert Booth had been of the opinion for some time that fusion was the only answer.

I had known Herbert for a number of years, and had a high regard for his ability and knowledge, and for his work industrially, politically and educationally in the county over many years, but on this issue I and many others throughout the coal-field disagreed with him. You could not be negative. I recall at this particular meeting speaking against fusion and putting forward a suggestion to extend the struggle to the whole of the Barber-Walker pits, thus making it a Company struggle.

Following the resignation of Herbert Booth as President, I was nominated for the position, and by a vote of the Branches was elected. This lasted only a few months, for the amalgamation of the two Unions did take place. So I was the last president of the Nottinghamshire Miners' Association, which had been founded in 1880.

In April of 1937 the ballot of the whole of the British coal-field, authorized in January, was taken by the Miners' Federation. Meetings were held and leaflets distributed throughout the coal-field. The leaflet explained that the Federation had sought to achieve a peaceful solution to the difficulties in Nottinghamshire by merging the two Unions, but the terms of the Spencer Union were not satisfactory. They were terms that could not be accepted by the great free body of mine-workers in this country. The miners were advised to vote 'yes' to the Federation's recommendation, which meant, if necessary, the calling of a national strike of the miners. There was a large majority in favour of a national strike to enforce recognition and the right to choose their own organisation.

Taking the ballot in Nottinghamshire was as difficult as it had been nine years previously. As in 1929 there was no access to Colliery premises, but it was taken in spite of the physical difficulties. The Federation decided on the outcome of the ballot that notices should be handed in to expire on 22 May 1937. On 6 May the Federation decided to suspend the notices for two weeks in response to an appeal from the Prime Minister, Stanley Baldwin. This was a disappointment certainly to the men at Harworth, and there was a feeling that this meant further discussion for the amalgamation of the two Unions. And this was so.

The Secretary for Mines was now in the business, hoping to avert a national stoppage. However, initially there was failure and on 6 May the National Executive made arrangements for a national stoppage on 29 May.

Between 6 and 28 May events moved rapidly. A neutral Chairman, Mr John Forster, was appointed, and provisional terms between the owners and the Federation and the Spencer Union were negotiated. These were accepted by a further conference, and this time the notices were withdrawn, and the Federation officials, with the Nottinghamshire Miners' Association, were to take steps to give effect to the amalgamation terms. This was not well received at the conference. There was criticism at what had been done, and the recommendation by the Executive to the conference was challenged. Frank Collindridge, a friend of mine, who was a Yorkshire member of the National Executive and in 1938 became Member of Parliament for Barnsley, said at the conference that the acceptance of the terms put the ballot vote at defiance. These sentiments were echoed by many in the coal-field, and by no-one more than the men at Harworth.

The end of the difficulty had not yet arrived in spite of the accepted amalgamation. Some members of the Nottinghamshire Miners, who had been so loyal during the ten lean years, were disappointed and refused to contribute to the new amalgamated Union. At Harworth, there was the greatest disappointment, for work there was available immediately for only 350 of the 1,000 or more who had been on strike. One of the terms of the settlement was that up to 350 names were to be drawn out of a hat and these were to be given employment. This was conducted in the Miners' Institute on Sunday afternoon by William, later Sir William, Lawther, President of the Miners' Federation, by Mr W. Cook, conciliation officer at the Mines' Department, and myself. It meant, and we were only too conscious of it, that at least initially 650 were to be disappointed. For the men at Harworth who had fought and struggled for Trade Unionism, it was not a happy ending. They suffered frustration and disappointment and the victory was only partial.

The demand for coal from 1934 was increasing. A change was taking place in the economic climate owing to rearmament, for the international sky was darkening; events in Germany were casting shadows over Europe. The threat and possibility of a national coal stoppage was possibly alarming the Government. Nothing had happened so far as the Nottinghamshire position was concerned until the eruption at Harworth, but there was the possibility of a national stoppage to resolve the problem, and then, through the Secretary of Mines, the intervention and appeal to the Prime Minister. Reflecting over the years I have speculated in my own mind, that had the war of 1939 taken place two years earlier, or had the situation in Nottinghamshire dragged on for two more years, it is conceivable that the circumstances of amalgamation might not have arisen. I do not think a miners' strike in order to obtain recognition from the owners and the right to join the Union of the men's own choice would have been tolerated. Who knows? The way in which it ended could have been different.

The situation in Germany, with the rise of Hitler, and his Fascist regime, the Spanish Civil War, the rise of Mussolini in Italy, and a situation of instability in Europe, made possible

Stanley Baldwin's appeal in 1937 for the position in the Nottinghamshire coal-field to be resolved by the parties to the dispute. Should there be a war in Europe coal would be in great demand for at that time it was a monopoly fuel. Oil had not 'penetrated' to any great extent. With an inadequate supply of coal, industry would have been unable to meet the demand that would arise. A strike in the coal-field would have been disastrous. That was why the Government showed itself at last interested enough to bring the parties in the dispute together.

And so the dispute at Harworth, after a long, bitter struggle, with all the suffering, arrests and imprisonment, was resolved. It was a struggle in the historic traditions of the Trade Union Movement and particularly the miners : a struggle that will have a place in history, long after the generation of the 1930s has vanished. It deserves importance for the men and women were magnificent : courageous and determined to make possible the right to organise in the Union of their choice.

The two Unions were dissolved and the Nottinghamshire Miners' Federation Union, part of the Miners' Federation, came into being officially on 1 September 1937.

CHAPTER VIII

After Harworth and Amalgamation

The ten-year dispute between the Nottinghamshire coal owners and the Spencer Union on one side and the Nottinghamshire Miners' Association and the Miners' Federation on the other, together with the Harworth dispute, came to an end in June 1937. The terms of amalgamation to which I referred in the preceding chapter were by a majority vote, accepted by the Miners' Federation at their delegate conference. The fusion of the two Unions as the solution to the Nottinghamshire problem and unity of the Federation, now able to speak and negotiate for the industry nationally was accepted by all the parties in the dispute. This kind of ending aroused mixed feelings; many were disappointed; some resentful. These feelings were expressed not only in Nottinghamshire, but throughout the British coal-field. Many who had hoped and struggled for the elimination of the Spencer Union never thought that fusion would be the final outcome, and immediately expressed their doubts and fears about it. I was myself disappointed at the outcome after ten years of hoping, and working and believing that fusion of the two Unions would never come. To say the least my immediate reaction was distasteful, but the majority at the delegate conference had so decided. With many others I accepted it, because it was impossible to do otherwise. There was neither the means nor the opportunity to continue, the Federation having decided under the circumstances prevalent that amalgamation was the solution to the problem. The argument for and against had been stopped and amalgamation of the two Unions, and the creation of one Union had triumphed. The disappointment and resentment was not one-sided, however. There were some members of the Spencer Union who were opposed to amalgamation for reasons different from those of the Federation and the Nottinghamshire Miners' Association. They were content to go on, feeling time was on their side. They had, too, on their side the coal owners, who at this time had economic power in their hands. Whatever the degree of dissatisfaction and from whatever quarter, amalgamation had come about, and it was the hope that unity, in the long run, when the wounds had healed, would be restored in the Nottinghamshire coal-field. Immediate concern was for the Harworth men whose names were not among those drawn out of the hat. There were 600 to 700 whose immediate prospects for employment were not rosy. An undertaking was given that as many as possible would be absorbed as quickly as the pit was capable of taking them. In the meantime some found employment at neighbouring pits and some returned to their native Durham; but it was a few months before the pit and the village returned to normal.

The negotiated terms of the amalgamation provided for a change of name for the new Union. It was to be called 'The Nottinghamshire and District Miners' Federated Union' and it remained as such until 1944, at which time the National Union of Mineworkers came into existence with its national change in structure and organization. The Nottinghamshire Federated Union became the Nottingham area of the National Union of Mineworkers and so remains.

The terms negotiated and agreed and accepted were that there should be five full-time officials, three from the Spencer Union and two from the Nottinghamshire Miners' Association. John George Hancock, who had been a full-time official of the Nottinghamshire Miners' Association for many years, up to 1926, went over to George Spencer on the formation of the new rival Union. For reasons of his own, he decided to retire—I would judge his advancing years were the main reason. This retirement left four: Val. Coleman, William Bayliss of the Nottinghamshire Miners, George Spencer and Horace Cooper of the Spencer Union. Who was to make up the number to five? In the shadows was Herbert Booth, who was not a full-time official of either Union as were the other four. Before leaving the Council meeting he had for many years been a very active member of the Nottinghamshire Miners' Association, and became its President. He was also the Nottinghamshire member on the National Executive of the Miners' Federation. After his resignation, there were rumours as to his membership of the Spencer Union. But I cannot vouch for their accuracy. The fact is that by agreement between the parties, Herbert Booth became one of the five full-time officials. George Spencer was President, Val. Coleman, General Secretary, Horace Cooper, Financial Secretary; William Bayliss and Herbert Booth, agents. These appointments were to continue for life or until retirement. Their successors were to be elected, as was the practice, by a ballot of the membership in the coal-field. George Spencer and Val. Coleman retired together in 1945 and their successors, D. J. Ley and Harry Straw, both of whom were stalwarts in the Nottinghamshire Miners' Association for many years, were the first full-time officials to be elected by ballot of the new Nottinghamshire Area Union of the National Union of Mineworkers.

Another matter of importance in the machinery of the new Union was that the Presidents of the two Unions were to be Vice-Presidents of the new amalgamated Union and be a part of the new delegate Council. This affected me personally as the out-going President of the Nottinghamshire Miners' Association. The other was Ben Smith, the outgoing President of the Spencer Union. This arrangement was to operate for a period of two years, at which time there should be only one, to be elected in accordance with the rules. Ben Smith, who was a much older man than myself, retired and, at the end of the two-year period, I was elected each year until 1941 when I retired and became Member of Parliament for the Mansfield constituency, thus ending my active association with the Union. The officials at the Branches were to be of equal numbers from each of the two Unions by agreement between the full-time officials. They were to hold office for two years, after which elections were to take place in accordance with the rules. The two Unions took a ballot of their members on the proposed terms, the result of which was reported to the

1. Father and Mother, hard-working parents, to whom I owe so much. Many memories of them I cherish. Appreciation of them continues to grow. What they were and what they did, often in trying and difficult circumstances, evokes feelings of gratitude.

2. North Lodge Farm. The place where my parents met in 1879. Mother was hired in Newark market-place, and Father in

3. The cottage in Mansfield Woodhouse where I was born, recently reconstructed, and now providing amenities and sanitary facilities non-existent at the time of my birth.

4. Sunday School Teacher, Albert Fell, the coal miner, who influenced my life and thinking more than anyone. A great, good man whom I shall remember with abiding gratitude.

5.   My wife. Brought up together in the Sunday School and Chapel, in 1921 we married.
For more than fifty years we shared the rough and the smooth.

6. The school. The first local authority school in Mansfield Woodhouse, built in 1903, where I was a scholar until 1908.

7. **Sherwood Colliery.** The pit where I worked underground for about twenty years, from a door trapper to the coal face. From 1909 until 1941 my working life was connected with this colliery.

THE BATTLE OF HARWORTH VILLAGE

First aid in the dance hall after a midnight battle—in which police were almost overwhelmed by strikers—in the colliery village of Harworth (Notts). Trouble started when men going to work on night shift were met at the colliery gates by strikers. Left: Mrs Wheeler shows the broken windows of her home.

"Chain Gang" Off to Work

MEN who are continuing to work through-out the strike for trade union rights at Harworth, marching on duty through the night accompanied by an escort of police. They have been nicknamed "chain gang" by the strikers, among whom bitterness has grown as their long fight goes on.

8.   Cuttings from the *Daily Mirror, Daily Herald* and the *Chronicle*, 26–27 April, 1937.

Some of the 31 men charged in connection with incidents at Harworth—scene of the colliery strike—on Friday night, leaving Worksop Gaol with Councillor Buckley, their secretary, after being remanded on bail yesterday.

MINERS TELL OF TROUBLE

MR. BERNARD TAYLOR, the newly-elected president of the Notts Miners' Federation (right), and Mr. Ronald Kidd, secretary of the National Council of Civil Liberties, taking statements from Harworth miners after the trouble.

Sir Stafford Cripps, defending solicitor in the Harworth disturbances charges, arriving with Lady Cripps at Worksop Court.

9. General Election 1945. My first contested Parliamentary Election.

10. Parliamentary delegation to Poland in 1946.

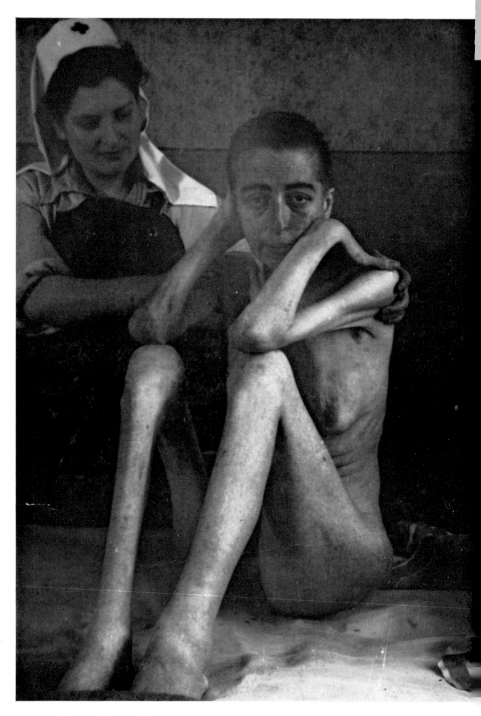

11. Conditions in Poland, 1946.

12. Labour Hall, Mansfield Woodhouse. The first home of the local Labour Party in 1932.

13.   My last election in 1964.

14.   Owen Ford at ninety years of age, still interested in the coal industry. Reading E. Page Arnot's *The Miners*.

15. Jesse Farmilo. My predecessor as checkweighman at Sherwood pit.

16. Charles Brown. My predecessor in Parliament for the Mansfield Division from 1929 to 1940.

17. Frank Varley. Official of Notts Miners Association and M.P. for Mansfield 1924 to 1929.

18. Val Coleman. General Secretary of Notts Miners Association, also of the amalgamated Notts and District Miners Federated Union.

19. William Bayliss. Official of the Notts Miners Association and the Notts and District Miners Federated Union.

20. Herbert Booth. President of the Notts Miners Association, and official of the new amalgamated union

21. German Abbott. Checkweighman at Rufford Colliery and Branch Secretary at Rufford.

22. George Spencer. Founder of the breakaway 'Spencer' union.

first delegate council of the new Union, and the necessary majority was given, accepting amalgamation.

This was the beginning of a new chapter in Nottinghamshire and for the Nottinghamshire miners. At the first Miners' Federation conference after the amalgamation, held in July 1937, Joseph Jones, the President, welcomed George Spencer and Horace Cooper to the conference with these words: 'In the name of this Federation, I extend a cordial welcome, and express the hope that they will continue their co-operation with us to the full, to ensure that the remaining parts of the agreement are fully carried out at Harworth.'

One of the resolutions at the conference was a protest at the prison sentences imposed upon our Harworth comrades, and especially the one on the miner's wife, Mrs Haymer. Both George Spencer and Horace Cooper voted for the resolution.

I was chosen by the Parties to be the Secretary of the Sherwood Branch, providing I obtained employment at the pit. One of the accepted terms of the amalgamation was that the officials of the Union would use their best endeavour with the owners to secure employment for those who had been the subject of discussion between the parties. This meant the collectors of the Nottinghamshire Miners' Association. The Nottinghamshire coal owners undertook to give favourable consideration to any representations made. I was not sure as to my future until towards the end of June 1937 when I received a letter from Val. Coleman, the General Secretary of the new Union, drawing my attention to the undertaking of the owners, and asking me to approach the Manager of Sherwood pit with a view to employment.

I presented myself along with Sydney Cook, another collector. I had memories of nearly eleven years before, when I was seeking to be re-employed. It was very different this time. The meeting with the manager, Mr C. H. Heathcote, brother of the General Manager who had treated myself and others so impolitely, was very cordial. We knew each other quite well, and, during the ten years on the few occasions we met, our conversation had been quite friendly. One of our infrequent meetings was at the occasion of the opening of the new pit-head baths in 1932 by the Chairman of the Sherwood Colliery

Company, Mr F. N. Ellis. I had an invitation as a member of the Mansfield Woodhouse Urban District Council. I attended and met the Manager who expressed his regret at the circumstances, and said that if he could he would be delighted to have me back at the pit. He further expressed the hope that one day the whole business would be settled. It was the first time I had met him in his office at the pit for ten years. He said he had been expecting us, and that in anticipation of our visit, he had been looking round the pit. He had found that there was an old airway that needed making wider and he thought this work would be suitable for us after being away from the pit so long. Sydney Cook and I thought it was quite magnanimous of him to be so thoughtful and we accepted the offer, signed on, and once again we were actual pit-men and employees of the Sherwood Colliery Company.

This now entitled me to maintain membership of the Union, and to act as Secretary of the Sherwood Branch. I had some difficulty about when to start work for I was President of the Nottinghamshire Miners' Association and I estimated that I would be called upon to attend the annual conference of the Miners' Federation. The check-weighman would be taking their holiday and as one of the sub-check-weighmen, with Sydney Cook, I would be required to deputize. I did not see the possibility of starting before August. I brought this difficulty to the Manager's notice. In reply he said, 'Of these matters I am not unaware. Sign on now, get your name in the book, and start when you are ready!' 'One other matter I should raise,' I said. 'You know I am a member of the Nottinghamshire County Council, and this takes up two to three days a week. The meetings are during the day, and I do not want every week to be coming to you or the under-manager for permission to be away from work.' 'Look, Bernard', he said. 'All these things I am aware of. You have my permission to make a start at your convenience, and to come when you can, consistent with your public duties.' It sounded like a fairy story, but it was true.

I started work and went down the pit again in August 1937. It was a new experience after stepping off the cage on 30 April 1926. Arriving at the pit bottom, I met my old friend

Albert Parr to whom I referred in an earlier chapter. He was now the over-man, a position next to the under-manager. He said, 'I have to take you to the place where you are to work.' We walked along, reminiscing. He expressed his pleasure that the wounds had been healed, and that I was back.

Up to this point I had not seen the under-manager. This was most unusual as it was the usual practice for him to do the setting on. It was the Manager I had seen; he had been assigned the job of finding employment for Sydney Cook and myself. I was given every facility to carry out my Trade Union work as Secretary of the Lodge, also my local government duties as a member of the Nottinghamshire County Council, and Mansfield Woodhouse Urban District Council. Not so much as a straw was placed in my way. The Sherwood Company and management carried out their undertaking not only to the letter but in the spirit of it too. Symbolically speaking, the one regarded as the prodigal was welcomed back.

In my mind at this time was a conversation I had in 1932 with a local policeman the morning after golden-voiced Charlie Cross had been killed. After telling me of the fatality, he said, 'I was talking recently to some one you know very well, Mr Stirland, the under-manager, and he was referring to you in a not very complimentary fashion. He said you had been "a bloody fool".' That was in the very early thirties. But there were no longer hard feelings when I resumed work, and, if my future was to be in the pit, I was pleased that the employment was to be at Sherwood where my working life, with the exception of twelve months, had been spent. I knew the management and the men. My future could have been different if I had had to seek pastures new in some other occupation. It was strange working underground again, but as this was the only kind of work I had done from a boy to earn a living and I was now forty-two years old the strangeness soon passed. I was home again, among many pals. Naturally the events of the previous ten years were often the topic of conversation: men could, and did, talk with greater freedom.

As one of the two Vice-Presidents of the new Federated Union, I became, with the full-time officials, a member of the newly constituted district Wages' Board. At the first and subsequent meetings of the Board, discussions took place on the question of a Pension Scheme for the Nottinghamshire Miners who came within the ambit of the wages ascertainment. There was then no National Scheme and no national agreement on wages. Each County Union had its own Wages' Board. This was a body comprised of the coal owners and representatives of the Union, which met monthly. The balance sheet of the industry would be presented to the Board by the accountants : proceeds from the sale of coal and the costs of production which included many items. What was left after deduction of this cost was to be divided on the basis of 85% to wages on the basic rates and 15% to profits, with a minimum of 38% to wages. In 1937 the industry was in a period of reviving demand, compared with the long period of depression in the late 1920s and early 1930s. It was prospering and this revival in the coal industry's fortunes was revealing itself by the payment of higher percentage on basic rather than the minimum of 38%.

It was in these circumstances, in the initial stages of the new Wages' Board, that the idea of a pension scheme found favour. Agreement was reached by all the members of the Board that a pension fund should be established, drawing its funds from the proceeds of the industry. I must in justice say George Spencer was a keen and strong advocate, and so the first and only one of its kind in the whole of the British coalfield was established.

The initial payment was five shillings per week to retired and retiring miners covered by the ascertainments in the Nottinghamshire coal-field. Over the years the fund has prospered, and the payment is now thirty-five shillings or two pounds per week. This pension is restricted to the miners in the Nottinghamshire coal-field and is additional to the pension of the National Coal Board which began after the nationalization of the industry in 1947.

Continuing as Secretary of the Sherwood Lodge and being one of the Vice-Presidents of the Union, now in the ranks as a working miner, I was able to meet the management once again to discuss and iron out any difficulty and to negotiate in person about the problems characteristic of mining life and work. There was evidence among the full-time officials at the monthly Delegate Council meetings, among the Branch officials, that they meant to make it work. I accepted the amalgamation, and, having done so, regarded the new set-up as another chapter in the history of the Nottinghamshire coalfield. I felt it was incumbent upon me if not to forget the past at least to forgive, and to devote my energy and enthusiasm towards making the new Union an effective and important unit of the national body—the Miners' Federation. The past was behind, the future in front, and there was a lot of work to be done.

The first task was to build up the membership. This was by no means easy. So many men were out of the Union as rivalry and bitterness had produced non-Unionism on a big scale. Disappointment and resentment were still there—so were the wounds and sores, and they took some time to heal. Painful memories lingered, but gradually the position improved, and membership steadily increased as the memories of the previous eleven years, impossible to obliterate, receded slowly into the background. The men, by a gradual process, came back to the Union, realizing, I believe, that unity was the way to progress.

In 1938 a new circumstance arose for me. An old friend, Jesse Farmilo, with whom I had worked in the Lodge at Sherwood for many years, and also in the political field, suddenly died, while we were talking at his home. It was a shock. Prior to amalgamation, he had, for many years, played an important part in the Nottinghamshire Miners' Association and in the Labour Party too. He was one of the founders of the Mansfield branch of the Independent Labour Party in the early 1900s. He had been an Alderman of the Nottinghamshire County Council for many years. He was a check-weighman at Sherwood pit and his passing created a vacancy. I was deputy check-weighman, having been elected in 1925. Sydney Cook was the other. Between 1926 and 1937, Jesse Farmilo had many a day off which had helped Sydney Cook and myself financially. Although barred from the colliery premises, we had legal rights under the check-weighers' Act and the management were unable to deny us access to the check-weigh box, the place close to the mouth of the pit where the tubs, full of coal, were weighed and registered by the weighman for the company. These check-weighmen acted on behalf of the men who had produced and filled the tubs with the coal and were paid by the men. The death of Jesse Farmilo created a vacancy. I was nominated for the job, and by a ballot vote was elected. After resuming work underground in 1937, I became, twelve months later, check-weighman at Sherwood Pit.

Check-weighmen in those days and years before, were regarded as the only free men at the pits. They were in the employ of the men, and were paid by the weight of mineral that came to the surface in tubs or little wagons. When workers came along the roadway from the working places to the pit bottom, exchanges would take place between the men in different 'stalls'. To use a bit of Nottinghamshire pit dialect the exchanges would be, 'How many tubs hasta sent out today?' The stalls were areas of coal worked by anything up to a dozen men. Nowadays the areas are from two to four hundreds yards in length; there are no tubs and all the coal is mechanically conveyed. Check-weighmen have now gone out, and payment is by measurement.

In the days before mechanization, the check-weighman, generally an official of the Lodge, and regarded as spokesman for the men, was free and without any inhibition or fear. He could talk freely with the management. My good friend, Jim Griffiths, at one time President of the South Wales Miners' Federation, and from 1936 to 1970 Member of Parliament for Llanelli, told a story which illustrates the standing and importance to the miners of the check-weighman: a miner in Monmouthshire had been caught taking some bits of timber home from the pit—not an uncommon practice. He was summonsed. At the time a check-weighmen at one of the Monmouthshire pits had been appointed a magistrate. Bengy, the offender, went to see him, and was shown into the parlour. There sat Isaac, the check-weighman and magistrate. Bengy told his story and asked Isaac what he was going to do about the summons. 'Look, Bengy!' said Isaac in reply, 'Of one thing you can be absolutely certain. At the Court you will get British justice.' 'Damn!' said Bengy. 'I don't want that. I want to get off!'

At the pit, and in the community, the check-weighman, especially if he was a local official of the Union, was the first person to whom the men went with their problems. It was a position of importance and responsibility.

I had been check-weighman only a few weeks before I had a breakdown in health. This was disappointing and frustrating. I am certain that this was caused by the strain at Harworth : so much speaking, many anxieties, and a lot of travelling. There was nothing organically wrong with me. I was medically advised that it was nothing but sheer nervous exhaustion. I was away from duty as check-weighman, and my Union activities suspended. This lasted for a number of weeks. In June 1938, my mother died. This was a great loss to me. She had always been helpful and a source of encouragement. My father had died two and a half years before. The 1930s were a decade to remember! However, in January 1939, I was able to resume my work and activities. I was now in a settled job as check-weighman and was in a different world compared with all that had happened since 1926. I was looking forward to a life of usefulness : serving my fellow men at the pit, in the Union, in Local Government, and in the political Labour movement, but this merits a chapter to itself.

CHAPTER IX

Politics and Political Education

In an earlier chapter I made a reference to my joining the Independent Labour Party in 1919. This was the beginning of my active identification with a Socialist Political party. Before this I had no active connection with any political party. The name of Keir Hardie and his writings attracted me. His pacifism, his work for peace, and his belief in the Brotherhood of Man, made a special appeal to me. I discovered I was more enthusiastic than knowledgeable and had a lot to learn in the sphere of politics, but I found comfort in the fact that knowledge is not a sudden impulse but something that is acquired through reading, study and experience. I had learned this in the Chapel, and it was no less true in the wider sphere of politics. I enjoyed my membership of the I.L.P. immensely. The meetings and discussions were helpful and the social activities I found pleasurable. The members, the majority of whom were older than myself, were good people and always helpful, and I found from them a welcome and encouragement. I soon concluded this was my political home, among people of like minds, with the same ideals and enthusiasm and an endeavour to translate them into realities through political action.

At the meetings we would express our emotions and ideals in song:

'England Arise,
The long, long night is over
Faint in the East
Behold the dawn appears.'

and Blake's 'Jerusalem'.

Another favourite was Symonds's:

'These things shall be. A loftier race
Than ere the world hath known shall rise,
With flame of freedom in their souls,
And light of knowledge in their eyes.'

The circumstances of those days provide nostalgic memories and are still, in moments of meditation, a source of inspiration and a part of my life that I treasure. I am grateful for the privilege of recalling them as a part of Life's Journey.

Many members of the I.L.P. of those days who did so much for the cause of socialism became public representatives on local authorities. The tide for Labour participation was on the swell locally as well as nationally. The day had dawned when Labour politics and Socialism were no longer dirty words.

In 1918 the Mansfield constituency was taken from the Liberals and won for Labour. In the early and middle 1920s seats were won on a big scale in local government. Mrs Wainwright, a stalwart of the I.L.P. was elected to the Mansfield Borough Council, and later to the Nottinghamshire County Council. In the former capacity she was Mayor, but her most outstanding achievements were in the field of education. She was dedicated to education and thoroughly mastered the subject, and was regarded as an expert nationally. Others were Mr and Mrs Marriott, the latter of whom became Mayor of the Borough of Mansfield; Eli and Elizabeth Hather, two wonderful people, the latter alive as I write, nearing ninety, so talented—a pity she had not had the opportunity of an extensive education! She was what she was—able and knowledgeable from her experience; German and Mrs Abbott, the former of whom became a prominent member of the Mansfield Borough Council, and three times its Mayor, are also still with us, over eighty years of age: Albert and Ivy Rhodes, the former of whom became a member of the Mansfield Borough Council; Tom and Mrs Whalley, who had a brilliant son, Eric; he went to Spain in the Civil War of 1936 and did not return. Politically he had a great future before him, and to his talents and ability I pay a tribute and revere his memory.

D*   93

His bones whiten in Spain as one of the fatalities of the 'International Brigade'. Tom Mellor, who recently died, over eighty years old, migrated from Carlisle at the end of the 1914-18 war. We had a lot in common politically. He had been a member of the I.L.P. for many years, and regarded his sphere as recruiting members. He was responsible for recruiting me. There was Lily Iball, now County Council Alderman Mrs Hill, who, as a young girl, was a very active member; there were also Harold and Mrs Woodward, Charlie Melbourne, all Trojans for work in furthering the cause of Socialism in Mansfield. I regard my membership of the I.L.P. as the nursery of my political education.

It was a thriving branch and a lot of preparatory political educational work was undertaken by all the people I have mentioned, and many others who sowed the seeds, the fruits of which are evident today. What was done helped considerably to awaken political consciousness, and make the Mansfield constituency the Labour stronghold it is now. From 1885 to 1918 Mansfield was a stronghold of the Liberal Party, up to which time it was part of the North Nottinghamshire Division. The Member of Parliament for Mansfield from its inception was always a Liberal. The first to be elected was Mr Carver Williams, a Gladstonian Liberal. In 1895, the year of my birth, Colonel Foljambe became the Member and remained so until 1900, when he was succeeded by Sir Arthur Markham until his death in 1916. He was succeeded by Sir Charles Seeley until the first post-war election in 1918, when the seat was captured by Mr Williams Carter, the Labour Party candidate.

My parents had always been Liberals and I recall that at every General Election from 1900 to 1910 my mother always pinned on the lapel of my coat a piece of yellow ribbon, the Liberal colour. This was also the routine at every County Council Election. At every one of these elections, my mother and her sister had terrific rows about Liberals and Tories. Verbally they fought like Kilkenny cats. My parents were not active members of the Liberal Party, but in thought and outlook they were radicals. After the election of 1918 and until their deaths at every election they supported and voted for the Labour candidate, and were overjoyed by the victory of William Carter. They regarded it 'The dawn of a new day'.

With the victory of William Carter, the Labour Party as distinct from the branch of the I.L.P. gathered momentum, and membership increased, and, as an organization, it gradually superseded the Liberal Party. It was a new experience to have a Labour Member of Parliament and the way to preserve this was to build up and strengthen the organization, and increase the membership.

In Mansfield Woodhouse there was a local Labour Party, but with the enthusiasm after the election and with an influx of young enthusiasts, a resuscitation of the Party was needed. This took place in about 1922. Albert Wilcox became the Secretary and myself the President. The membership increased; it was not difficult to recruit members; the fee was small—one shilling per year—and there was strong enthusiasm for the cause. A lively Local Party was built up, and became an important part of the Mansfield Divisional Labour Party. The General Election of 1923 provided a disappointment for the Party, however. William Carter was defeated ostensibly by a Liberal—but in fact he crossed the floor of the House of Commons to join the Tories almost immediately. It was a short Parliament. Frank Varley, a full-time official of the Nottinghamshire Miners' Association, was chosen as the Labour candidate, and at the 1924 election was successful, and became Member of Parliament. So Mansfield was again represented in the House of Commons by the Labour Party. But this too was short-lived. Frank's health failed and, in March 1929, he died. Charlie Brown became the candidate and at the General Election became Mansfield's Member of Parliament.

Prior to this election I had, in 1927, become the Secretary of the Divisional Labour Party, and acted as Agent in the election of 1929. This was entering into pastures new and a new experience for me. I found it interesting. There was one difficulty—funds were far too low for contesting a General Election which is an expensive business if the job is to be done properly and efficiently. The contributions of the Nottinghamshire Miners' Union had dropped considerably. There were two reasons for this: firstly the membership of the Union had dropped since the stoppage of 1926; secondly, the operation of the Trades' Disputes' Act of 1927 meant that members of the Union had to contract in to the political fund of the Union, instead of contracting out (there was little disposition to do the former). This affected adversely the contributions from the political fund of the Union to the Divisional Labour Party. The election financially was run on a shoe-string, and the money was raised by donations and collections at meetings. These were very well attended. There was no television and the people attached importance to the spoken word and the exposition of the Party's programme, but the candidate was not sponsored by a Trade Union, as was the case with William Carter and Frank Varley and, apart from a donation from the National Party, we were on our own in raising the money to finance the election. It was not an easy matter. People had little spare cash; the wages of those working allowed so little surplus, and many were unemployed. It was a worry, but what was lacking in cash was compensated for by enthusiasm. A lot of voluntary work was done, not only by the active Party members but by others who came forward to offer their services. If poor financially, their political fortunes were rising. With every passing day during the period of the election campaign, one could sense a victory for Labour.

We won by a handsome majority. Although industrially from a Trade Union standpoint we were weak, politically we were strong. It was an opportunity for the miners to show where their loyalties lay, and they certainly did.

The Labour Government was formed with Ramsay Mac-Donald as Prime Minister. It lasted for two years only and then there was another election. It was too soon after the last to give us time to recover financially. The national economic circumstances had their political repercussions. There were defections among some Labour Ministers, and at this election in 1931 the situation was novel, for the issue was between National candidates, a combination of all the Parties, and the Labour candidates.

In Mansfield the Labour candidate was Charlie Brown again, and the National candidate a local solicitor, Mr E. B. S. Hopkin, who had the support of the Tory and Liberal Party organizations. Again our funds were meagre; again I was the election agent. We went into the contest with the odds heavily against us. There were scares and bogeys galore, and the leaving of the ranks by people like Ramsey MacDonald, Philip Snowdon and others did not help politically. But we retained the seat by a substantial though reduced majority. A mere handful of Labour members had returned to Westminster and we in the Mansfield Division congratulated ourselves, and rightly thought we had won a magnificent victory.

Between 1931 and 1935, the year of another election, the third in six years, I had a busy time politically, addressing meetings, raising what funds we could to carry on political activities in the Division, and preparing for the next General Election. In 1934 I was asked to be the candidate for the Calverton Division in the County Council election. It was a pretty hopeless position for Labour but it was estimated that the propaganda in this almost rural area would be valuable. The sitting member, Mr Thom Shipside, was a local man, a Liberal and a good man. He was the son of a blacksmith in the village of Oxton in Nottinghamshire. I am told that during the Boer War, the family had had difficulties with the local squire, for whom they did a lot of work such as shoeing the horses and repairing the agricultural implements, the major part of a village blacksmith's business. The Shipsides like many Liberals were pro-Boer and because of this, the squire refused to do any further business with them, so the son, Tom, started a cycle and repair business and this was the beginning of what eventually became huge business with the advent of the motor car. He became the sole agent for Morris cars in the Midlands area. I recall that on the day of the election, he had one hundred cars at his disposal. I lost, but did very well indeed. During the count I remember Tom saying to me that it looked like being a near thing. I did better than expected, and was not disappointed. The purpose of doing a little propaganda had been achieved. The meetings were well attended in the villages, and Labour's message was well received. Today there is a colliery in Calverton, with a substantial mining community. Passing through, as I do occasionally, I hardly know it, but the experience of 1934 remains.

97

Between 1931 and 1935 I had a busy time politically; life was full, addressing meetings, raising funds to carry on political activities and preparing for the next General Election. A friend, Fred Hubbard, had recently joined the Party and become the Treasurer for the Divisional Party. He was a railway clerk, employed by the Midland Railway Company. In raising money he was first-class, and he was also good at husbanding resources. A bazaar was planned, and he did the major part of the organizing. A considerable amount was raised—in the region of £200. This sum was something we had not had for years. We thought it an El Dorado which would be a great help when the election came.

At the General Election of 1935, Charlie Brown, an extremely good Member of Parliament, was the Labour candidate for the third time, and I again acted as the election agent. Funds, whilst in a better state compared with the previous two elections, were still inadequate. We still needed to economize, and I decided the election addresses should be cut on stencils, and turned off a Gestetner machine, manipulated by hand, so as to economize on the cost of printing. Also, at the end of the day, the Party would have the machine for the future. It was a gigantic task, and I thought the end of running off the required number of 35,000 would never come. Albert Wilcox, myself, and others worked like Trojans. Time was limited; so much had to be done in two weeks in order that the Post Office should have the addresses ready for distribution to the Electors. In retrospect I doubt if I would embark on such a project again. Our hopes for another victory were high, our fear of defeat less than in 1931. The political climate was different: no Post Office Savings' scare and no defections. At the end of the day we had our reward: Charlie Brown was elected with a handsome majority. This was the third time of asking, three victories in a row. It was compensation for the work put in by so many people.

In 1937 I gave up the secretaryship of the constituency party as Union activities and Local Government work had become increasingly demanding. I was succeeded by an admirable colleague, Charlie Davey, whose work for the Party was praiseworthy, and I am unable to do adequate justice to him in words. His life and activities were, however, impaired by failing health. I brought him to Manor House Hospital in London to see a specialist, a friend of mine, Sir John Nicolson. The report was not good and shortly afterwards he died, quite young, in his early fifties. His passing was a great loss to his family and the Labour movement in Mansfield.

During the early thirties I was approached by the Newark constituency Labour Party to become prospective Parliamentary Candidate. I met the Executive but I declined the offer. It was impossible for me financially to visit the area of the constituency, which was large, and the Party was unable to meet the expense.

In December 1940 there was a staggering blow for all of us : Charlie Brown died. His passing was a great loss to the Mansfield Division and to the nation. He had been a good, industrious Member of Parliament, and had served the Mansfield constituency and the Labour Party admirably. His death to me personally was a great loss. I regarded him as my mentor and adviser. We had been associated politically for many years. Together we had experienced the difficulties of the early post-war period, the coal stoppage of 1926 and the depression of the late 1920s and early 1930s. Together we were members of the Board of Guardians and the Nottinghamshire County Council. For me it was the end of a chapter. I had lost a great friend for whom I had a high regard and affection. His death was for the Mansfield Divisional Labour Party, too, the end of an era. In the short period of twenty-one years, there had been three different men as Labour Members of Parliament. For the fourth time in twenty-one years, another choice had to be made. In a succeeding chapter I will tell of the choice, for I became personally affected.

In Mansfield Woodhouse, we had a lively, enthusiastic Party. All the members were proud of it, but we had no meeting place. The homes of all the members were too small, with the exception of one member, Randolph Parker, who had a much bigger room than most people. Here, and sometimes in the Baptist and Congregational premises, we met without fail every month. The enthusiasm for a meeting place of our own was bubbling over. The senior member of the party was Joseph

Wilcox, a man who in service to the public of Mansfield Woodhouse, did more than any person I can think of. He began to raise money in order to provide a home for the Party, and he succeeded. Where many others in this sphere would have failed, he, by his own methods, his own schemes, and his own efforts, raised more cash than anyone towards the provision of a building.

In 1931 the Party decided to take the plunge; there was enough money to purchase a site. A plot of land was available, but there was a strong possibility of a refusal if it were thought the Labour Party wanted to buy. A member was chosen to make the purchase in his own name, after reporting the price. This he did and the deeds were then transferred from him to the Party.

The work of clearance of the site and the foundations were carried out by voluntary labour, and of this there was no shortage. The members worked hard and long for it was no small undertaking. Cash was still a problem, but eventually a wooden new building was erected on the hire-purchase system. We now had a home of our own and there was great rejoicing on the day of opening in 1932.

The membership continued to grow, activities increased, and we were a happy family. The debt was soon liquidated. The building was, and still is, a monument to so many who did so much work and gave so generously. In time and money, sacrifices were made to make the venture possible. Recently the building has been enlarged again by voluntary efforts of the members. Bill Smith has been the moving spirit in this latest venture and every credit must go to him and many others for what they have accomplished. The building has been, over the years, a place for educational facilities, political discussion and activity and social activities, and many men and women have enjoyed the fellowship. The years in this period of political activity were interesting and exciting. The men and women with whom I worked and had fellowship are a part of treasured memories. Together we worked and did our utmost to advance the cause of socialism and Labour politics in Mansfield Woodhouse.

In the early post-war period there was a growing demand

for education in political, economic and political philosophy. I myself was ravenous for improving my knowledge politically. The activities of the National Labour College movement after the war was extended into the provinces. This educational organization began in 1908; how it began is an interesting story. Trade Unions had a practice of sending some of their promising members to Ruskin College by awarding scholarships. The Principal was Denis Hird. One of the students in 1908 was Frank Hodges from the South Wales coal-field. A strike took place in this seat of learning, the outcome of which was the founding of the Labour College Movement. It began with premises in London, accommodating full-time students, and it was financed by the South Wales Miners' Federation and the National Union of Railwaymen. Many whose names are household words in the Labour Movement began their careers at the Labour College in London: James Griffiths, Anuerin Bevan, Will Mainwaring and many others, all of whom played an important part on the political stage, and some of them became Ministers in future Labour Governments. This educational body did excellent work for the Labour Movement. I myself was not a full-time residential student at the College but with the extension of its activities, as it began to bring opportunities for education into the provinces, I was delighted to take advantage.

The country was divided into organizational areas. In 1922 a class was started in Mansfield Woodhouse. The organizer for the area, a big one comprising the counties of Nottinghamshire, Derbyshire, Lincolnshire and Northamptonshire, was Charlie Brown. He was also one of the tutors and for a number of years took the class in Mansfield Woodhouse. He was a good lecturer. His knowledge of economics, industrial history, contemporary politics, and other subjects including political philosophy was profound, and he could make it so simple and easy to understand.

The members of the local Labour Party regarded this innovation as wonderful—the discovery of a new world in the field of learning. Here was something providing a new experience, and full advantage was taken of it. A number, including myself, to this day willingly acknowledge a debt of gratitude for the benefits received from the tutorship of Charlie Brown. To me he was no stranger, for I knew him well as a Methodist lay preacher up to the end of the First World War. We were on the Methodist Local Preachers' plan at the same time and I frequently met him in this capacity. In the course of the classes, he introduced me to many books and I found the reading and study of them of great help in my pursuit of knowledge. I think about them even now and still, when opportunity affords, go back to such books: *Ancient Society* by L. H. Morgan, *Easy Outlines of Evolution* by Denis Hird, *A Worker looks at Economics* by Noah Albett, *Industrial History* by Mark Starr, *Positive Outcome of Philosophy* by Deitzken, and books by Jack London, Upton Sinclair and V. L. and Barbara Hammond. The tuition at the classes and the books recommended advocated socialism and knowledge. These were sources of information: to all of us it was new and revealing. With my limited opportunities I was overjoyed by this privilege afforded by the Labour College Movement.

Classes in and around the Mansfield area became so numerous that it was impossible for Charlie Brown to take all of them, and others stepped in and undertook the job as lecturers. I was asked to take a class at Huthwaite on 'Industrial History'. It was a new venture for me and, although willing, I was conscious of my shortcomings. I found during the discussions that there were men who were not only older but so much more knowledgeable than I was. I managed, however, and benefited from the experience. I think the members of the class did too. The National Council of the Labour College has every reason to be proud of the work it did in the field of working-class education. It made knowledgeable socialists and equipped them with information that has stood them in good stead and made them more effective in their work for the Labour Movement.

During the period 1930-31 I was awarded a two-day a week scholarship by the Miners' Welfare Committee to Nottingham University. The course was enjoyable and I derived great benefit from it, but I was handicapped because I had so many activities in the industrial and political fields that I was unable to give the time to do the necessary study in order to obtain the maximum educational benefit. There were meetings every evening, and at the time I was Chairman of the Mansfield Woodhouse Urban District Council, in which capacity I was for the period a magistrate, and so there was not sufficient time for me to give the detailed study I would have liked. Nevertheless, I found the lectures on Economics, History and English very helpful. The books provided with the scholarship, which I still have, were a treasure and are still a pleasant reminder of the few months I spent at Nottingham University, and the many people I met. I was and still am grateful for my brief excursion into the academic world. A few years ago I told Anthony Crosland, a good friend who had a brilliant academic career and was a Minister in the Labour Government of 1966, that I envied him the opportunity which had come his way educationally. Magnanimously he replied, 'I envy you the experience you have had. Remember, experience is a good tutor and schoolmaster.'

CHAPTER X

Local Government

From the beginning of my entry into active politics, local government had an attraction for me. I was of the opinion that there should be greater active participation by the working class through the medium of the Labour Party. This view was growing inside the movement and was producing results.

In the middle 1920s, Labour Party Candidates in the industrial areas of the country were capturing seats from all kinds of people: Tories, Liberals and Independents. This was so in the area in and around Mansfield; the working class was increasing its numbers on the local authorities. For the Labour Party the sun was high in the political sky; the administration of local government from a representative standpoint was in a process of change. For so long it had been the preserve of the Tories, Liberals and Independents. (Whatever the latter meant was anybody's guess!) The working man was entering the Town Halls and offices of the local authorities in effective numbers for the first time. In some circles they were regarded at first as intruders and the bringing of politics into local government was thought undesirable, but as their numbers grew and their contribution appreciated, this feeling soon disappeared. The local Labour Parties, after the First World War, contested the elections with their Labour Candidates and were successful. This is fully accepted nowadays, particularly in the industrial areas. References in the press, on television and radio, in announcing the results take this form: 'Labour win or lose control of the named local authority' or 'the Tories have met a similar fate'. There is now a sharp, clear, political representation on the local authorities. People from different areas in the country interested in local government invariably ask what is the political complexion of your authority. And in the Councils, particularly in the larger authorities, the members divide on political lines when it comes to matters of policy.

In Mansfield Woodhouse, the local Labour Party made its selection of candidates for the local authority, which was, and still is, an Urban District Council (and to which I shall refer later) from nominations of the affiliated bodies such as Trade Unions, and this method still continues.

In 1925 I was nominated by the Nottinghamshire Miners' Association and selected as a candidate by the local Party to contest a seat on the local Council, and also one on the Mansfield Board of Guardians. At the elections, both on the same day, I was elected to both authorities. I found my first entry into this field of local government (a new experience) extremely interesting and, the longer my membership of both bodies continued, the more I enjoyed it. The kind of administration between the two was so different, although each dealt with people and their problems. I discovered I had a lot to learn in order to become what I wanted to be, an efficient and sympathetic administrator in the sphere of local government.

The Board of Guardians at this time did not have a good public image among the population. There were uncomplimentary remarks about the Workhouse Master, not personal, but about the office. I remember a bit of doggerel about him and his Christmas pudding but it is a little too rude to quote here. The workhouse was always called 'the Grubber'. The dread of this place was common and there was justification for this. The Relieving Officer, one of the symbols of the Institution, was regarded with no more affection but rather with fear, particularly among those who had no alternative but to apply for outdoor relief; and many had to apply because of sickness, however proud and reluctant they were. My mother's family was an example. A particular section of the community, the elderly, always had a nagging fear they would end their days in 'the Grubber'. As the shadows lengthened, with life ebbing away, the cry often was: 'Save me from the Grubber'. Such poverty was not, in a general way, self-inflicted, as often these people were so accused, but because they had never had sufficient money to have a decent, reasonable standard of living, and they were consequently totally unable to provide for their eventide. The prospect of the workhouse was a nightmare and always lurking in the background of the mind. If not this, there was the Relieving Officer, with his questions and enquiries.

The Board met fortnightly—a statutory requirement—and on this day the whole of the premises, which were extensive, had to be inspected by the members. At Mansfield there were three sections : the Hospital, the Institution or workhouse, and the casual or vagrancy wards, as they were often referred to officially. The patients in the hospital were the 'Geriatrics' and the chronic, incurable cases, who were very sick, bedridden and waiting for the end—they had gone there to die! The treatment was neither preventative nor curative ; it could not be otherwise. Senility, mental and physical and malignant disease made them impossible to cure. All that could be done for such people was nursing, and help with drugs and medicine to make their remaining days tolerable and comfortable, and this is what happened.

Nevertheless admittance to the Poor Law Hospital at that time and for many generations before was not a pleasant prospect.

The workhouse, or institutional part of the premises, was different. Here was accommodation for the mentally subnormal, not physically impaired, and for those who needed protection, because they were unable to take their places in the outside world. Also there were the elderly who had no home. Sometimes in cases of this kind a man and wife were separated. There was one part for males and another for females. There was also a part for the vagrants or casuals who wanted nothing more than a night's shelter and breakfast before they moved on again.

At no time did I find the visitations pleasurable. This was an aspect of life that I found depressing and my tender human sympathies and susceptibilities were wounded. I felt deeply that there was need for change in this social field. I had read some of Dickens's writing but now I saw conditions myself at first hand and I realized that only the fringe of it had been touched; there was the greatest need for a break from the tradition of the Poor Law which had been in existence from the time of Queen Elizabeth I in the sixteenth century.

I have many memories of those days as a member of the Board of Guardians and I retain one in particular. The incident happened in 1928 or 1929, during the dark days of the depression, the days when unemployed men were brought by the Insurance Officer of the Employment Exchange before the Courts of Referees on the charge of not 'genuinely seeking work'. As I was going through the vagrancy ward one Thursday morning, I saw a man scrubbing the floor; it was the usual practice for the vagrants to have such a task assigned to them by the Workhouse Master. I bade the man 'Good morning!' He rose from his knees and returned the greeting, so politely. My immediate reaction was that he was not a vagrant. An interesting conversation developed. He was a single man who had been before the Court of Referees; his unemployment benefit had been disallowed. He was a ship's draughtsman from the shipyards of the north-east. He told me he was unemployed, had no prospects and no 'dole'. He did not want to stay at home and be a burden. He was making his way to the hop fields in Kent to earn a few shillings. I wished him well, which was poor comfort, and bade him 'good morning' and 'good fortune'. I have often wondered how he fared; and he was one of thousands in the same predicament.

Concerning Courts of Referees and 'not seeking work', many experiences came my way. One episode I remember of a man who appeared before them. First, the Chairman of the Court said to the appellant, 'Where were you looking for work yesterday?' 'Pit so-and-so', said the man. 'What did the Manager say?' asked the Chairman. 'As usual, full up,' he replied. About every day of the week the Chairman asked the same question and the Manager at every pit visited gave the same answer: 'Full up'. One day, in desperation, the appellant said, 'Sir, I had come to the end, fed up and frustrated. So, after six days and no hope, I went to the river fully determined to end it all. Off came my coat and hat, ready for the plunge into the deep, dark water, when a voice from the river shouted

"Full up". Sir, it is everywhere the same—"Full up".' These were the days of the depression. I thought again of the man, the ship's draughtsman—what a waste of talent and ability!

Additional to the visits and inspections concerned with the Board of Guardians there was the Relief Committee, dealing with the applications for 'outdoor relief' as distinct from domiciliary relief. The Relieving Officer would submit the information given by the applicants and the Committee would decide how much to give. This being done, the question of the liability of relatives, mainly sons, would be raised by the Officer. From this there was no escape; it was a statutory requirement. The Officer had all the information, after having made extensive enquiries from the liable relative. If there was ability to pay, an order had to be made, and this was enforceable in the Courts if not paid. Often the magistrates had this kind of case before them. I recall one man in particular. At one time we had been at Sherwood pit together. He had a son, whose marriage had broken down, and there was a young child. The father had left Mansfield Woodhouse and could not be traced. The mother applied for relief and an order was made on the grandfather who was a liable relative of the child. I recall him saying that he would not pay and would be prepared to go to prison. The making of orders on liable relatives was an irritation and often caused family estrangement.

In 1928 I was again elected for a three-year period to the Board of Guardians. This, however, was cut short by legislation in Parliament. In 1929 the Local Government Act abolished Boards of Guardians, transferring their power to the County Boroughs and County Councils for administrative purposes. Public Assistance Committees in the County Borough and County Councils were created, and the term 'outdoor relief' was changed and called 'Public Assistance'. Theoretically it was a change but in practice the administration was much the same; it was a change in transfer, not in practice, but a change in personnel certainly. The Board of Guardians, centuries old, were no more and passed into history. Its passing was a foretaste of the changes that were to come in eighteen years' time, with the enactment of the National Assistance Act in 1948.

The area of the Board of Guardians in Mansfield, or the Mansfield Union as it was known officially, was extensive, embracing the council areas of Mansfield, Sutton-in-Ashfield, Mansfield Woodhouse, Kirkby-in-Ashfield, Warsop, and Blackwell Rural District Council, a densely populated area. To omit referring to Joseph Wilcox would be remiss. He and I were the two representatives on the Board from Mansfield Woodhouse. He was a great man, full of sympathy and the milk of human kindness, much concerned with the problems of the elderly, the sick and the poor. His work for the people of Mansfield Woodhouse, and the public service he rendered are his monument, and many, including myself, have every reason to remember him.

Service on the Board of Guardians was a revelation of the problems and afflictions of people. To be able to do something, however small, to help to alleviate them, was in itself a compensation, and of one thing I am certain, whatever natural sympathies one might have had, this kind of public service was an avenue where sympathy and understanding of the people could be practised. I am not only grateful but consider myself fortunate for the opportunity, so early in my public life, of having this experience from which I learned so much, and which has been of inestimable value over the years.

I became a member of the Mansfield Woodhouse Urban District Council in 1925 and remained as such until 1946, when I decided at the first post-war election not to seek re-election. In the twenty-one year period I contested five elections and was successful. I was proud to have been a member of the Council of my native place. I had witnessed its growth, and in twenty-five years the population had increased to 14,000. There were two collieries and a textile mill. These undertakings, with household property, made up the rateable value which, of course, with any grants from the National Government, determined how much money there would be to spend on the public services. The product of a penny rate for the size of the place was small, only £168. The total revenue from rates to the Councils was not a large sum. From it two-thirds had to be paid to the County Council. This was usual for the District Councils within the counties and not exceptional to Mansfield Woodhouse. The remaining one-third was for services for which the local Council was by statute responsible, such as parks, some highways, sanitation, refuse collection, water supply, housing and fire services. In the twenty-five years prior to 1925, population increased from 4,877 to 14,360. The product of a penny rate in the same period rose from £4 to £168. The population increase of one-third and the financial resources by one-quarter meant that the financial position had not kept pace with the increased population. The rise in population meant additional responsibilities, and a greater need for more not less money. More people with a growing social conscience for expanding the public services needed more resources. There was much to do and too little money.

In 1925, the year of my advent, the complexion of the Council changed. There was a Labour majority. Those of us entering local government for the first time were in sympathy with the manifest growing desire for improvements in social standards, and were full of determination and idealism to improve social standards in the Public Services.

Many are the memories of my membership of the Local Council. I recall one in particular. The Fire Service was a bit of a joke. The meagre apparatus was mounted on a two-wheeled carriage. If and when needed, it was drawn to the scene of the fire by hand whether the distance was far away from or near to the depot, where the carriage was kept. Often before the men arrived on the scene it was too late. Fire, like time and tide, waits for no man; it is a good servant but a bad master. On the new Council, I was keen and determined to stop the joke, and we did. An up-to-date fire engine, motor drawn, with fire appliances was purchased, in the hope it would not be required but, on the other hand, if wanted it was there. A fence at the top of the cliff is better than an ambulance at the bottom! The fire service was manned by the employees of the Council. The luxury of a full-time service was financially impossible. The men gave good service, underwent training and were always on call. The service remained with the Council until the outbreak of war in 1939, when it was taken over by the Regional Fire Service. The importance of an up-to-date Fire Service is now universally recognised as important. It is now part of the County Council administration in conjunction with the Home Office, and every part of the country is covered.

Another urgent matter in 1925 was sanitation. Mansfield Woodhouse was an old-world village, and there was an urgent need in the interest of public health for conversion to a water carriage system for its sewage. This was tackled as a priority; new sewage works were installed, and improvements were made progressively. Within a few years the Council was in a position to state proudly that, with the exception of outlying farms and a few properties, there was a complete water carriage system. The time of the night soil-cart had ended. This was an advance in public health, a step in the prevention of infectious diseases. I then thought, and still do, that expenditure on prevention was much more important and outweighed the cost of curative measures for typhoid and other diseases which were not only expensive but caused so much suffering. How satisfying it was to know that the ashpits and the pail closets, breeding ground for flies in abundance, and disease, had been relegated to the limbo of the past! I regarded this achievement in the sphere of sanitation by a small authority with limited financial resources very satisfying.

I was made Chairman of the Council in 1930. This appointment carried with it a seat on the Magistrates' Bench. By virtue of the office one became a Justice of the Peace. This system continued until 1967 when it was abolished by Act of Parliament. No longer, outside the City of London, are Mayors of Boroughs and Chairmen of Urban and Rural District Councils eligible to sit as Magistrates by virtue of such offices.

The question of superannuation for the employees of the Council was a hobby-horse of mine. Superannuation for local government employees prior to 1937 was optional. Mansfield Woodhouse was among those who had not exercised the statutory optional provisions. Prior to superannuation becoming compulsory, the consent of the Authority and the employees was necessary before a scheme could be established. In the early 1930s, perhaps 1932, discussions started with the employees. The Council was willing, also the non-manual workers, but there was difficulty with, and opposition from, the manual workers. This was understandable as wages were low, if regular, and a further deduction from the wage packet was anathema. I recall meeting them and saying that what was good for the officials, who were willing to take advantage of a superannuation scheme, was good for them too. They were persuaded, and the scheme came into operation in 1932. Recently in conversation with an ex-employee of the Council, now retired, and a beneficiary of the fund, I was told how grateful he was. After almost forty years, the conversation reminds one of the couplet : 'Bread cast on the waters shall be seen after many days.' Many of the employees were delighted when they retired, that the superannuation scheme had been started way back in 1932—now forty years ago.

Membership of the Local Council was a satisfying experience and a good training ground for whatever the future might have. I walk around the place now and see things which today are taken for granted ; but they had a beginning and, when initiated, almost fifty years ago, they were looked upon with suspicion by some. From some quarters came the remark, 'Those spendthrifts on the Council, they should have their heads looked at, spending public money on such a project ! It is sheer waste !' Improving the public services with a view to making people happy and part of a community is my idea of the purpose and function of local government. It is a costly business but the provision of services and amenities for the welfare and enjoyment of the people is essential.

In the mid 1930s the office accommodation was becoming increasingly inadequate. The population was expanding and as a consequence the administrative work was growing and 'staffing' had to be increased to deal with the situation. Housing was an expanding matter in local government administration and the Council was anxious to do the utmost to the maximum of its financial resources. Full advantage was taken of the post-war Housing Acts of Parliament, particularly the Wheatley Act of 1924, and the Greenwood Act of 1930, the latter dealing with slum clearance. The system of 'Direct Labour' was instituted. All this meant more administrative work and more staff. The then existing office was bursting at the seams. It was an old building purchased from the Wesleyan

Methodists whose chapel it was—the place I had attended as a scholar in the Sunday School and later as a member of the Chapel. As the Council Offices from 1911, and when I became a member of the Local Council fourteen years later, it had memories for me. It was here as a small child, a toddler, that I began. Now I was helping to decide policy for the whole of the local community and taking decisions affecting the lives of 14,000 people.

The old building, having served two purposes for many years, was no longer adequate or suitable as public offices. At the time one of the oldest buildings in Mansfield Woodhouse, a private residence, occupied by the Chairman of the Sherwood Colliery Company, was offered to the Local Council. It was known by two names; by some it was called the Castle, by others the Manor House. Whatever name it was given, everybody knew what was meant. It is an Elizabethan building beautifully situated in extensive grounds. At one time, during the seventeenth century, it was the home of Sir John Digby, who was on the side of the Royalists during the Cromwellian War. The Colliery Company who offered the place to the Council for £1,500 wanted the Council to purchase it in order to preserve it as a bit of old Woodhouse. It was a generous gesture by the Colliery Company and I have no doubt they could have disposed of it for a much greater sum. The price was very low, but, as with all old buildings, to adapt it for administrative purposes would mean a heavy cost. Some in the Council said it would be better to start from scratch with a new building, an argument difficult to contest. I, however, supported the purchase, which I have never regretted. It preserved for posterity a bit of old Woodhouse, and has provided a good administrative centre. Its fate might have been in the hands of speculators: it might have been demolished, which would have been a pity.

My twenty-one years on the Local Council were excellent training. There were responsibilities but also privileges, one of which, the most precious, was to meet so many people who were keen to develop and improve public services for the benefit of the community.

The year 1934 was another landmark in my 'Life's Journey'.

At the County Council election, my friend, Albert Wilcox, was successful in Mansfield Woodhouse in winning the seat from a local doctor, Mr Palmer, who had been the County Councillor for a number of years. Labour's star was in the ascendancy and shining brightly. To take the seat from the local doctor who was highly respected and well liked was a good victory. Albert Wilcox, at the first meeting after the election, was made an Alderman, which caused a bye-election. I was chosen as the candidate to succeed him which I did and was returned unopposed. I remained a member of the Nottinghamshire County until 1946. There was only one election between 1934 and 1946. Owing to the war of 1939 to 1945, all elections, local government and parliamentary, were suspended. At the first post-war election I did not seek re-election because I was a Member of Parliament. My wife, who was a County Councillor for the other ward, transferred to the ward I had represented, and was successful at the 1946 election. Later she became an Alderman and so remained until her retirement in 1967.

Half of the eleven years of my membership of the County Council were in the period of the war. The latter half of the eleven years was full of administration of a routine nature. No new projects, such as highways and school buildings, were possible. These could not be undertaken because of shortage of labour and materials. All we could do was to make the best of what there was. The work of the committees and the administrative work went on during the period of the war.

One of the two committees to which I was appointed, in 1934, was the Mental Hospital Committee. Membership of the County Committees was decided by a body, selected by the County Council. For many years, since the inception of the County Councils and, until 1948, and the passing of the National Health Act in Parliament, Mental Hospital administration was the responsibility of the County Councils in the county areas. The hospital for Nottinghamshire was situated at Radcliffe-on-Trent, twenty-five miles from Mansfield Woodhouse. The journey was either by train or bus to Nottingham, then by car to and from the hospital, a distance of ten miles. The meetings were held monthly. All the business of the various committees and of the general meeting, to whom the committee reports were submitted for approval or otherwise, was carried out on the one day. It was a full day. I had to leave at 8.30 a.m. and did not arrive back until 6 p.m. Lunch was provided, however, and I admit to looking forward to the horseradish sauce always provided with the beef! The statutory requirements for visitation were similar to those of the Board of Guardians. The monthly inspection of the extensive premises and seeing the many patients, at least 1,000, were obligatory.

My feelings were mixed—sadness that so many people were afflicted with mental illness, and pleasure that there was a retreat for these unfortunate people. For many, a cure was effected by rest and treatment, and many were able to take their place in the outside world. But there were many for whom there was no hope either of cure or recovery. At this time the majority of the patients were certified. They were looked upon and referred to as having been in the Asylum—mad or daft—and were to be kept at arm's length—a kind of social ostracism. Happily there has been a transformation in public attitude. The procedure is less rigid now. Today the majority of the patients, after examination and interviews at the clinic of the local hospital by a visiting doctor from the Mental Hospital, will be admitted as voluntary patients. Mental illness is no longer a stigma and is regarded in the same way as physical illness. This change in attitude among the general public, and the new medical approach, are more than welcome, and unfortunate people afflicted with mental illness are no longer regarded as lunatics and beyond cure, to be incarcerated for the remaining part of their lives. The dimension of the change is such that there are now national and local organizations interested in, and catering for, the mentally handicapped, both for the young and old. In the days of forty years ago, whilst seeing the need and hoping for this change, I often despaired that it would ever come, but it did!

The change of name from 'Asylums' to Mental Hospitals was a stage in the right direction, and no longer do the public regard these places as asylums in which to put people and lock them away from the public, but as retreats for treatment and nursing, where so many of them can recover and eventually take their places, again in society. Since I began my membership of the Mental Hospital Committee, there has been a change in the way a patient is received. No longer is certification a pre-requisite, but many people today are advised at the out-patients' department to undergo treatment and, of their own volition, enter the Mental Hospital. I know personally men and women who have responded and have been restored to normality.

My membership of the Committee together with the visitations so intensified my appreciation of the medical and nursing staff that I find it difficult to describe this adequately. They have a difficult and sometimes unpleasant job and need the patience of Job. Their forbearance and patience with difficult cases were wonderful and I have often remarked that it needed a dedicated person with rare qualities to enter the profession and be successful. Society is indebted to the staff in the Mental Hospitals for the love and care and skill they bestow on the mentally ill.

I had a few embarrassing moments when visiting the wards. Some patients often asked questions too difficult to answer. The most embarrassing moment I had was one morning when I was inspecting the female wards in company with other members and the Matron, a dedicated person to her profession. One of the patients whose hope of recovery was negligible, came up to me in the presence of the Matron and said, 'Do you know our Matron?'. 'Yes', I said. 'Oh, you do. Well, take it from me, she is a prostitute!' She said it in less polite language however. Had there been a mousehole, I would have made for it. The Matron so sweetly said, 'Minnie is not in a good mood today; it is one of her off moments.' I mention this to indicate the qualities of patience and reasonableness required in the profession of mental nursing.

Two other committees to which I was appointed were Education and Public Assistance. This latter committee was the successor of the now defunct Boards of Guardians administering the whole county and was responsible for the payment of outdoor relief and domiciliary services transferred from the old Boards of Guardians. I found my five years' membership of the Mansfield Guardians helpful in this new role. The County Council, on assuming the new statutory responsibility, adopted a decentralized scheme, and formed area sub-committees, the area covered being similar to that formerly administered by the Board of Guardians. This meant there was a sub-committee in Mansfield. The constitution of these sub-committees consisted of elected County Councillors and co-opted members, mainly from the District Councils. Their duties and responsibilities were delegated by the County Council, but were identical with those of the old Board of Guardians. There was a snag: the area committee in making its decisions respecting payments to applicants could be overruled by the Public Assistance Committee. This was unsatisfactory because revision of the awards was, in the majority of cases, in a downward direction. This veto was resented by the Area Committees, certainly in Mansfield. There was no scale rate, and where the Public Assistance Committee was of the opinion that the orders were too generous or too low, the orders were revised. In the Mansfield Area sub-committee many of our decisions were regarded as too generous and became subject to the hatchet at Shire Hall.

In the 1930s the applicants for 'outdoor relief' were numerically increasing, for, in addition to the elderly and the sick, there were the able-bodied unemployed. Either their unemployment benefit was exhausted or they had been before the Court of Referees, the majority of them being charged with not genuinely seeking work and their benefit disallowed. This applied to single men and married men with dependent families. After we had made our decisions, some of them would be revised by the County Committee for reconsideration. I do not recall one case asking for a revision upward in respect of the unemployed. We refused to accede to the request of the County Committee, and not a single case of the unemployed applicants did we change. Back to Nottingham they went, and the County Committee had the last and final word. The onus and the shame were theirs. There were many verbal battles and harsh words. Our disadvantage was that the Public Assistance Committee held the purse strings. In this period, with the threat of a veto hanging over you, it was a frustrating and disappointing job. Particularly from the applicants there were sorrow and sometimes plenty of cursing.

Many times my thoughts wandered to the ship's draughtsman, for he had said he had no dole and he may have been too proud to apply. Even if he had, as an unemployed single man, able-bodied, he would have been turned down for 'outdoor relief'. The single man of those days was faced with one of four choices: to be a burden on his parents, to take to the road, or the workhouse, or to end it all. I was told of an experience a friend of mine had in the north of the county. Early one morning he was taking a walk, and came to a stream where a man was washing. During the conversation it transpired that he was a single man, unemployed, with no dole, who had left home and taken to the road where he was living rough. He said it was a precarious existence. The sky at night was his ceiling and the grass in the fields his bed, and he went on to quote a few lines from a hymn in the Methodist hymn book:

'The foxes have holes, and the birds have nests
In the shade of the Cedar Tree,
But my couch is the sod, Thou, Son of God.'

There were many such tragedies in the 1930s.

There was a much more pleasant side to Public Assistance: the one dealing with the care of children, particularly children mentally and physically handicapped. This, like the service of 'outdoor relief', was a transferred service from the Boards of Guardians. Membership of the Education Committee was most interesting. This had developed into an extensive service, dealing with all ages from five up to entrance to the University. There was a number of sub-committees dealing with the many aspects of the educational system. I was a member of three: Attendance and Welfare, Special Schools, Sites and Buildings. The two former dealt with the problems of boys and girls of tender years, problems which were the concern of the parents too. The reports of the school attendance officers, dealing with truancy and other reasons why children had not been attending school were illuminating. The practice of truancy, however, was declining and absence from school for this reason was getting progressively less. There were cases when parents were summonsed and taken to Court, the Committee not being satisfied with the effort of the parents in getting their children to school. A summons was the last resort, and happily today there is little desire among children to play truant, and there is a keen awareness on the part of parents for their children to participate in the privileges of our educational system from the Primary School to the University.

In Nottinghamshire there were two special schools for 'educationally subnormal' children—children who were educable but had a low intelligent quotient. It was on the report and recommendation of the School's Medical Officer that the children with this disability were recommended for places, with the parents' consent. There were two special schools, both residential, one for girls, one for boys. An old friend of mine, County Councillor Matthew Holland of Selston, played a big part in this special provision for this type of child. Together, as members of the committee, we frequently visited both schools. It was always refreshing to see these children being given a chance and a tuition suitable to their restricted ability. Many of them were afterwards able to earn their own living and became independent, entirely because of the special provision made. The Headmistress of the Girls' School was Miss Foster and Mr Tomlinson was Headmaster of the Boys', and they had many years at the schools. Both were ideal people for this kind of work, and did excellent jobs for the county and the children. County Council work was absorbing and, when I left it, it was a wrench. For a long time there was something missing in my life.

In 1939 I was appointed a Magistrate. This office has been the least significant of my public activities, the main reason being that two years afterwards, in 1941, I became a Member of Parliament which restricted my attendance at the sittings of the Court. The Bench to which I was appointed was in the Division for which I was Member of Parliament. Here was a difficulty. I sought advice of the Lord Chancellor's Department. The advice given was that it was not illegal to adjudicate in the Division for which I was Member of Parliament but it was not looked upon favourably. I accepted the advice as I thought it right and did not attend the sittings of the Court. I only continued as a Magistrate because I found it useful for the signing of documents that only a Magistrate could sign. My experience as a Magistrate, therefore, was by no means extensive.

CHAPTER XI

Member of Parliament

In 1941 owing to the death of Charlie Brown M.P., there was a vacancy for the Mansfield Constituency in the House of Commons. It was wartime and, as in 1916, during the period of the First World War, there was a political truce between the Labour, Tory and Liberal Parties. This was honourably kept by the three Parties. In some constituencies where vacancies occurred, there were contested bye-elections because other Parties, not a party to the truce, and individuals, contested for the vacancy. This was, however, rare, and only happened occasionally, but it did happen.

The seat in Mansfield had been represented in Parliament by the Labour Party. The Tories and Liberals had no interest owing to the truce, and the Labour Party, of course, assumed responsibility for finding the candidate. The usual machinery was set in motion by the Divisional Labour Party which asked the affiliated bodies to make nominations. It was at this stage, which for me was the moment for making an important decision, that approaches were made by a number of Trade Unions, including the Miners, and also by local Labour Parties, asking for my consent to be nominated.

I confess the decision was not an easy one to make, for two reasons: I was now settled in a job as a check-weighman and was interested in the work of the Union. Naturally I was torn between two loyalties, the industrial and the political. It may seem strange, as at the time it did to me, that when my nomination from the Branches went to the headquarters of the County Miners' Union for endorsement by the delegate Council, George Spencer, now the President, whom I had got to know much better for I often met him at the monthly delegate meetings and at the Wages Board, called me into his office and sought to persuade me not to stand. 'You will be more useful in the Union,' I recall him saying. 'There will be late night sittings—I've had some and, believe me, they're no good!' I was not persuaded, any more than he had been in 1918, when he accepted the Labour Party candidature and the miners' nomination.

My name went forward to the selection conference of the Mansfield Divisional Labour Party with five others. They were Francis Williams, a journalist, ex-editor of the *Daily Herald*, Evan Durbin, author and a professor at one of the Universities, Percy Bairstow of the National Union of Railwaymen, Alderman Beck of Mansfield and Albert Wilcox of Mansfield Woodhouse Labour Party and the Derbyshire Miners' Union. Francis Williams did not turn up, leaving five to be interviewed. There were two ballots and I emerged successful, and became the candidate. The election was not contested and I was returned unopposed.

For me it was the beginning of a new chapter. In the country as a whole, there were more than thirty million electors represented in the House of Commons by 625 members. My thoughts were: 'What a privilege! One that can come to so few from amongst so many! To be at the centre of events, and to walk along the corridors and sit in the places where so many had been before, whose names are household words in the long history of the British Parliament!' I realized too that it was not only a privilege but carried with it responsibilities. Initially the thought occurred to me that I would be a stranger in a strange land, meeting new people, with fresh customs, in a totally different atmosphere from the one at the pit.

During the last week as check-weighman, I was asked to meet one of the directors of the Colliery Company. The conversation was most affable. He said how pleased he was that one of his workmen from being a young boy was now going to Westminster as a Member of Parliament. He suggested it would be his pleasure to give me a cheque for quite a reasonable sum. I asked him what for and he replied, 'to buy some clothes'. I told him I was grateful for his kind thought but I did not propose to dress up like lamb and lettuce because I was going to Westminster and it would be out of character. I thanked him for his offer. I was convinced the only thought in his mind was good and the gesture was a token of appreciation. I expressed regret in having to decline his offer, not on my part claiming any virtues, but I am sure he was disappointed.

The very last day at the pit, the Chairman of the Company asked me to call at his office. He was anxious in person to express his pleasure and to offer his congratulations. One of the customs at the pit from its inception was that the check-weighman had concessionary coal on the same terms as the employees of the Company, although the check-weighman was employed by the coal-face men. The Chairman said he would like that concession to continue. He said it was a pleasure to make the offer, adding it would be the means of keeping my name on the books. I expressed the thought that it was not necessary. He said he hoped I would accept, and I did and received this benefit, paying the usual price of five shillings per load, to a maximum of twelve loads a year, until Nationalization of the Coal Industry in 1947.

I received many letters and telegrams, also visits to my home by members of the Party and friends, and the local authorities congratulated me on my selection, and expressed good wishes for the future.

Having made arrangements with the Labour Party's Chief Whip, I departed to London: it was April 1941. On entering the Palace Yard, I was questioned by a police officer as to my business. Tom Williams, M.P. for the Don Valley in Yorkshire and later Minister of Agriculture, whom I knew quite well, assured the policeman that I was the new member for Mansfield. The police officer then directed me to the office of the Chief Whip, by whom I was well received, and made to feel at home. Here I went through a rehearsal of introduction, the usual practice for a new member coming in at a bye-election.

I recall that there were two of us to be introduced or 'sworn in' as it is called in the House of Commons. The other person was John Dugdale who had been elected for the West Bromwich constituency. With a sponsor each side of me, I walked up to the table, took the oath, signed the book and shook hands with the Speaker who was Captain Fitzroy. This was, and still is, the practice for a candidate entering after a bye-election as distinct from a General Election when there are no sponsors. Then the newly elected members sit on the benches and each individual row is called by the Speaker. The House was full and I felt all eyes were fixed on me. It was an ordeal and I was relieved when this first step had been taken. I recall that after signing the book and before being welcomed by the Speaker, I stumbled over the feet of Mr Churchill and Mr Attlee, both of whom sat side by side on the Government front bench. It was then a coalition Government. The former was Prime Minister, the latter his Deputy. It was the old House of Commons which, a month later, was completely destroyed by a German bomb. It was the last swearing-in of members in the old House of Commons. John Dugdale, now deceased, and I have the distinction, if it is one, of being the last persons to be sworn in to the old House of Commons. Immediately after the war it was rebuilt and opened in 1951.

After the preliminaries of being sworn in, I was welcomed by many members, not least by James Griffiths who had come to the House in 1936. As miners, we knew each other quite well but this was the beginning of a personal friendship that grew with every passing day. We had so much in common and our experiences were identical, and for thirty years at Westminster, we have remained close friends. I even now remember him relating to me his first day's experience at Westminster. James Maxton, M.P., one of the men from the Clyde, said to Jim Griffiths, 'Of course, you will need refreshments sometimes. There are two places, the bar and the tea room. My advice is: choose the tea room.' Jim Griffiths said, 'Good advice it was from an old Parliamentarian. Do tha' likewise!'

The House of Commons, like so many properties and people in London, was a war casualty. What could be done? Parliament had to go on and a fresh home had to be found. Church House, adjacent to Westminster, became the new 'House of Commons'. Eventually, however, we returned to the Palace of Westminster after an arrangement was made with their Lordships for the use of their chamber as the House of Commons. This continued until 1951 when the new chamber was available. During this period the Queen's robing room was in use as the House of Lords.

The first main preoccupation of a member is to make his or her 'maiden' speech. Until this is done, you do not feel part of the place, so the sooner it is done the better it is for the new member. It is expected of you in Parliamentary circles on this first occasion not to be controversial; on the other hand it is a tradition in Parliament that a member shall not be interrupted during his or her first speech. My maiden speech, which was in Church House, was about disabled miners and the provision that had been made in Mansfield for their treatment after leaving hospital. There were, and still are, many serious non-fatal accidents in the mining industry, particularly broken limbs, but the worst type of injury was to the spine. After weeks, even months of treatment in hospital, this type of injury was such that continued treatment was necessary but it took different forms. In the sphere of orthopaedics, medical opinion was focusing attention on the possibility of recovery or semi-recovery through occupational therapy and remedial exercises. The coal industry, through the joint efforts of the coal owners and the Union in Nottinghamshire and Derbyshire, established a centre called the Miners' Welfare Rehabilitation at Berry Hill in Mansfield in 1937. The person in charge of the medical side was Mr A. E. Nicol, a leading orthopaedic surgeon. The Mansfield centre was the first of its kind in the British coal-field. It was visited by representatives from all parts of the coal-field, and what was witnessed at first hand was so impressive and was obviously producing such beneficial results that similar centres were established in other coal-field areas. It has been my experience that severe paraplegic cases, regarded as hopeless in previous days and wheeled about in bath chairs for the rest of their days, have recovered to an extent that their mobility was increased to the point that they were able to walk unaided, and I have known milder types of paraplegia return to a lighter occupation. Many disabled miners in the Nottinghamshire and Derbyshire coal-field have greatly benefited from this remedial treatment. It was on this theme that I based my maiden speech. It may have been the first of its kind in the House of Commons. I felt it was important to call attention to what was being done in Mansfield and to express the gratitude of many disabled miners and to those, particularly Mr Nicol, who were working in this sphere. The Centre is still in existence. Its scope has been widened to include other than miners and it is now administered by the National Health Service as part of the hospital service.

During my first four years in Parliament, 1941 to 1945, it was the period of the war and there was a coalition Government. There was little legislation, few divisions and, what there was, was more or less non-controversial. Three Bills occur to me—all agreed measures. The first was the Disabled Persons' Bill which became an Act. It became known as the Tomlinson Act. It was a measure to make better provision for the disabled, particularly in the field of re-training. The numbers were increasing for, in addition to the industrially disabled and those handicapped from birth, there were the casualties of the war, those in the services and the civilian casualties from the bombing. It was a piece of humanitarian legislation, with economic advantages and the restoration of independence to individuals whose one hundred per cent capacity had been impaired, depriving them from returning to their normal occupations. Ernest Bevin, at this time in the House of Commons, as Minister of Labour, George Tomlinson and Mr McCorquodale, Parliamentary Secretaries, together brought a new vision and a new approach into the sphere of disability. The Tomlinson Act was a recognition of the just claims of the disabled, providing the opportunity for them to take their place in society, and prevent them from vegetating for the rest of their lives without hope of living useful and independent lives. The Tomlinson Act sowed the seed, the fruits of which are in evidence today.

I recall having a long conversation in 1942 with Ernie Bevin on the subject of disablement and what was being done at Berry Hill. What a vision he had! He was clear in his mind as to what should be done for bringing greater happiness to disabled people by ensuring their economic advantages. He realized something had to be done to prevent talent and ability being wasted and to preserve dignity and independence. The

Act of 1943 was the expression of his desire as Minister of Labour to do something for the disabled. In the closing speech of the debate he said, 'It is because I appreciate the importance of this question of vital manpower that I commend the qualities of this Bill as a means of preserving the virility of the nation and the productive capacity of every human being.'

I persuaded him to come to Mansfield to see at first hand what was being done at Berry Hill. He came and certainly was impressed both by what he saw and with the reports of Mr Nicol. After the inspection, a cup of tea was provided for the guests, one of whom baited Ernest Bevin, which brought out from him an outburst of humour in which everyone within earshot joined. The circumstances at the time were such that everybody who could do a job, even those with limited physical ability, were to be offered, and given, employment at some kind of job. The whole of the nation's labour power, both male and female, was being mobilized, as it was wartime. The gentleman, who was connected with the Midland coal owners' Indemnity Company, was complaining to the Minister of Labour (Ernest Bevin) that, in his opinion, the Employment Exchange was taking the utilization of labour a bit too far. 'Look, Mr Bevin,' he said, 'a man with impaired vision was sent to one of our collieries for work; it is really ridiculous!' 'Ah!', said the Minister, 'if I knew the vacancy officer, I would congratulate him. Maybe he thought there was a vacancy on the Board of Directors!' This was a spicy bit of humour and had the place rocking with laughter, much to the discomforture and annoyance of the man who thought he had scored a point.

Two other pieces of legislation during the war, under the Coalition Government, were the Education Act and the Family Allowance Act. Mr R. A. Butler was the Conservative President of the Board of Education and Mr Chuter Ede the Labour Parliamentary Secretary, both of whom had a wide experience in the educational field. They were opposites in their political views, but knowledgeable, and well fitted to be in charge of the Bill in the House of Commons, the purpose of which was to re-cast the whole of the law as it affected education. It was a measure to promote the education of the people and the progressive development of institutions devoted to that purpose, and to secure the effective execution by local authorities under the guidance and direction of the Minister of Education.

The new designation, as distinct from the President of the Board of Education, was to provide a varied and comprehensive educational service in every area. The debate lasted for two days and it was generally agreed that the Bill made great advances, but some said it did not go far enough. Others had reservations on matters like the Independent and Public Schools, and the denominational Schools. All of these bones of contention were well ventilated during the debate on the Bill. One other provision was a proposal to raise the school leaving age to fifteen. There was a provision in the Bill, described by Mr Butler as a further human aspect : the provision of meals and medical attention and treatment. He remarked, 'This is one of the Sections which appeals to me most because you actually see the worth of the investment in the children, not only in their growth but in their cheeks. The Government are taking fresh powers to impose this duty and will cause the milk and meals policy to expand and grow.' I wish some of Mr Butler's successors would read what he said in 1944. Then there would be less tampering with this important service. The tendency now is to restrict and make it increasingly difficult for it to grow and expand as was envisaged in 1944. Chuter Ede said it was the first comprehensive education measure ever presented to the House of Commons, comprehensive being the operative word. Before this there had, of course, been education measures before Parliament—long before my time— but on 19 January 1944, the day of the Second Reading, everybody in Parliament was agreed that the many proposals in the Bill meant a step forward in the educational field, so much so that there was no dividing the House.

There was also the Family Allowance Bill, which was a new venture, unlike the system of Education which was a progression. Family Allowances were a start in the field of expanding social services—a recommendation of the Beveridge Report in 1942. But the idea was not new. Long before the report by Beveridge, Miss Eleanor Rathbone, at this time a Member of Parliament, had advocated and campaigned for this for many years. Whilst not in charge of the Bill, as a backbencher she had the privilege of initiating the debate on the Second Reading. Her opening words were: 'I am regarded as the grand-mother of this proposal.' Aneurin Bevan referred to Miss Rathbone as the foster-parent of the scheme and is also en-titled to our congratulations. Miss Rathbone did as much as anyone inside and outside Parliament for the institution of Family Allowances. She was a justifiably proud person on 8 March 1945, but so humble about the many congratulations. Not everyone is the sower of the seed and then able to see it grow and blossom into fruition as Miss Rathbone did, and in historical perspective 'Family Allowances' are now accepted as an integral part of the social service structure and are a monument to her persistence and work. If only for this, I hope she will long be remembered. The main criticism of the Bill was that there was no appointed day for its operation and it was hoped that there would be no delay about this. It did not, in fact, come until the end of the war and after the General Election of 1945. These three pieces of legislation in the social field were a tribute to Parliament at a time when not only Parliament but the whole nation was preoccupied with the war, and physical damage, disturbances and upheavals were taking place among the population on an extensive scale.

Morning sittings were instituted and the House sat from 11.00 a.m. to 5.00 p.m. This was a departure from a long-established practice but was certainly advisable and it con-tinued until the end of the war when the usual custom was restored and still continues. Parliamentary practices continued. There was the usual one hour question-time to Ministers every sitting day (which was restricted to three days a week). There were many debates, some of them critical of the conduct and strategy of the war. There were also domestic matters: pro-duction of munitions and the evacuation of children from vul-nerable and exposed areas. Parliament, even at this time, was not without its critics of the Government, although it was a coalition comprised of all Parties. There was a number of secret sessions, when only members were present, and the Press and Public galleries were cleared for some announce-ment about the war to be made. These were not, as is the normal practice, recorded in Hansard, the daily official report of Parliamentary proceedings.

One memory I have was of General Smuts addressing both

Houses of Parliament. This could not be done in either House because none other than members can be in the House, let alone speak, when it is in session. The arrangement was made for it to take place in the Royal Gallery—a reasonably extensive area. It was filled with gilded, golden-coloured chairs. There was a narrow alleyway for the procession to walk down to the raised platform. From the ceiling hung powerful electric lamps which gave a wonderful effect. The place was full to capacity. Members of both Houses of Parliament were taking advantage of this unusual occasion. What impressed me most was the procession of so many who had been on the political stage for many years, some of them before I was born, men and women rich in experience and accustomed to the rough and tumble of Parliamentary life and Party politics like Smuts, Lloyd George, Churchill, Attlee, Bevin, Morrison, Amery, Greenwood, Butler and so many more. The whole audience stood until they reached the platform. Standing there, a very small pebble on the political beach and a new entrant to Parliament, I visualized some part of history was passing before my eyes with those present including Smuts, a Boer in the South African War, Churchill in the limelight and Lloyd George too of the same period. As time marches on, the more historical to me the occasion becomes. It is strange how some occasion rivets itself on your mind so that its freshness is retained and becomes a memory. This is one of many memories I still have and, every time I pass through the Royal Gallery, I see it all again.

I began to feel my way about the place with the help and advice of many members, particularly the Miners' Parliamentary Group, and I soon settled down. In this war period, London was not a pleasant place. The bombing and black-out were sources of anxiety and were unsettling. How the people of London endured it all was amazing and no words of mine can adequately portray the resources of courage they had and displayed. They certainly were in the front line of attack and to them I pay a humble tribute.

The doors of Parliament were never closed and its business went on undeterred under circumstances unprecedented in its long history, for, with the advent of aerial warfare, the country was vulnerable to attacks from the air. My main preoccupations were in the domestic sphere, taking part in debates on the mining industry, the Social Services and the asking of questions on a variety of matters concerned with the problems of constituents at home and matters from people in the services. The subjects did not lack variety and the number surprised me until I looked up the index of the official reports : Church parades in the army, billeting allowances, clothes rationing, food supplies in canteens, hearing aids, open-cast coal, Home Guard duties, pneumoconiosis and the industrial diseases. To these latter two, I shall refer again. Many of them were brought to my notice by constituents and the majority of them were peculiar to the circumstances of the war.

One matter in the domestic sphere that was of great importance both inside and outside Parliament was the publication of the Beveridge Report. It would not be exaggerating to say no matter has aroused the interest and curiosity of the British Public so much as this has done. Sir William Beveridge at the inception of the Coalition Government in 1940 was appointed by Arthur Greenwood, the Minister responsible for the Social Services, to report on the social and allied services, and to recommend proposals for legislation when the war came to an end. On the day of its publication, I remember walking down Whitehall and noticing a queue outside a bookseller's shop. I learned that they were waiting to purchase the Beveridge Report. I believe it captured the imagination and attention of the whole nation. Members of the Forces at home and abroad, and the civilian population, were discussing it privately and in public, and it became the basis of important and extensive legislation, affecting the whole nation in the early post-war period. To it I gave special attention and detailed study, addressing meetings on the proposals, and I found this stood me in good stead in the early days when the war ended. I shall say more about this in a later chapter when I refer to my experience at the Ministry of National Insurance. In the dark, uncertain days of the war it required vision to formulate the proposals, and optimism to translate them into legislative form so that they could become the law of the land.

In 1942, the Miners' Parliamentary Group, thirty-seven in

number, was uneasy about the restrictions in relation to compensation payments for a disease of the lungs known as silicosis, among coal miners. At the time, Herbert Morrison was Home Secretary and Osbert Peake, who later became Lord Ingleby, was Under-Secretary. Prior to 1948 anything connected with Workmen's Compensation was the province of the Home Office, after which it was transferred and became the responsibility of the Ministry of National Insurance. The Miners' Group raised the matter, and the ensuing negotiations were conducted with Osbert Peake, who was well fitted for the task as he was connected with a family who had pits in the Yorkshire coal-field, and was therefore knowledgeable on Workmen's Compensation and the mining industry.

After long negotiations, in which I took part, a change in the law was effected. Any person whose lungs were affected with dust other than silica dust contracted at his work at the mine would be entitled to compensation. The word coined was pneumoconiosis and, upon medical certification, a person whose lungs were affected by the dust, not only silica but other dust, was considered to be suffering from a recognized industrial disease—pneumoconiosis. After 1943 the term silicosis was not often heard, those victims to this lung affection being now referred to as suffering from pneumoconiosis. It was a step forward and it is now not as difficult for a sufferer to establish a claim as it was prior to 1943.

Another industrial disease was dermatitis. I had seen so much of this and witnessed distress among men, not only from the complaint itself, bad enough to endure, but often from agony of mind when a man was told by the medical referee that it was constitutional and not occupational. This state of affairs was the cause of mounting dissatisfaction in the Nottinghamshire coal-field. I asked questions about it and met the Home Secretary to try to persuade him to remove the distinction between occupational and constitutional dermatitis, for it meant so much to these men. The difference between sickness benefit under the National Health Scheme (or Lloyd George Benefit as it was referred to so often) and compensation was very wide. The latter was not more than thirty shillings per week until 1940 when the first increase was made to thirty-five shillings per week with allowances for children, and in 1943 when the maximum rates were again raised. The point I raised was that a man certified as suffering from constitutional dermatitis received sickness benefit which was much less than compensation. I was unable to get the Home Secretary to remove the distinction between the two definitions and make medical certification of dermatitis come within the scope of an occupational disease and therefore be compensatable. Many years have passed but, alas, the distinction still remains. Even today a person medically certified as having non-occupational dermatitis, receives benefit only for sickness.

The outcome of my questions and representations was a change in respect of who should be the medical referee in the case of a dispute between the sufferer's own doctor or one for his Union, and the employer's doctor. Up to this point the medical referee was a local general practitioner in Mansfield and this was the practice in other areas too. The Home Secretary appointed a dermatologist to act as medical referee in dermatitis questions and the men had to travel to Leicester for the examination. I recall asking the Home Secretary a question in the Commons on the appointment. The answer was that the person appointed was a dermatologist and the only man who had applied. Apart from the distance involved, the position was even less satisfactory than it had been with the general practitioner. The unfavourable decisions, at least, were as many, maybe more, than before the appointment. One man I remember well, had acute dermatitis. There was no dispute between his and the employer's doctor but there was a dispute as to what kind of dermatitis he had. To decide the issue, the man was summoned for examination by the medical referee. He made the long journey to Leicester. On his return home he told me that he had acute dermatitis but the decision was that it was constitutional which meant that he had lost the appeal and there was no compensation payable. John Timmons, Member of Parliament from the Lanarkshire coalfield, was having the same difficulty among the miners and he asked my opinion about the new arrangement in the Nottinghamshire coal-field. In the light of my experience, my advice to him was to continue with the practice of the medical referee being a general practitioner.

The change had not solved the problem nor reduced the

dissatisfaction. Men working in high temperatures and dusty conditions are susceptible to this skin disease and no one, not even a doctor, can convince a man that his condition is not due to high temperature and dust. I have known men whose condition, after a short period away from heat and dust, has cleared up. They have returned to work but the outbreak has occurred again within a few days. To tell the sufferer that he has dermatitis but that it is constitutional makes him not only frustrated but sceptical and makes him think every man's hand is against him.

In October 1943 there was a Bill dealing with Workmen's Compensation to increase the rates, raising the ceiling of maximum payment. Herbert Morrison, the Home Secretary, introducing it among other things, said it was a temporary measure pending the introduction of a new and more comprehensive scheme. I had the privilege of speaking in the debate. I ended by saying these words: 'The time has arrived in our social history when this vexed question of compensation, with all the miseries consequent upon the present law, when a person's earnings have been interrupted either by industrial disease or accident, should be faced. It is time that this House took its courage in its hands and made absolutely sure that in future all the mitigating circumstances should be considered when a man falls by the wayside as a result of circumstances over which he has no control, and that better, broader foundations shall be laid upon which a decent structure shall be built, and whereby justice shall be given to the unfortunate injured man.' Implicit in these words was my experience of the past and the hope for the future. At the end of the war some of the hopes materialized and fundamental changes took place to which I shall refer in a later chapter.

The atmosphere in the House of Commons during the period of the war was sometimes deep with sadness when an announcement was made. Pearl Harbour, the loss of a convoy plying its way on the high seas, casualties from aerial attack—these occasioned sombre silent moments when deep emotions were stirred. There were reports of casualties in the deserts of Africa and reports from the Eastern Front where Russia was facing the onslaught and attack of the German Forces. Often the Prime Minister would come to the House and give us information on the conduct and progress of the war, either in public or secret session.

One memorable day on the afternoon of 8 May 1945, the Prime Minister came to the House of Commons to announce that the previous morning at 2.41 a.m. all the German Forces had surrendered and hostilities would officially end at midnight on 8 May. Mr Churchill moved a motion to which no one else spoke : 'That this House do now attend the church of St Margaret to give humble and reverent thanks to Almighty God for deliverance from the threat of German domination.' The silence in no way signified the absence of thankfulness. At that moment all had an inner feeling of gratitude that the carnage and killing of the past almost six years had ceased.

Immediately after the announcement, the Speaker, preceded by the mace which, during the sittings of the House had rested on the brackets, symbolizing that Parliament was in session, led the procession from the Palace of Westminster into the Church. The procession was a long one, members of both Houses taking part. The service was simple and short and, at the end of it, the members walked back in procession. The bells of the Abbey were ringing out their peals : crowds of people were expressing their thankfulness by cheering. The long dark night with its uncertainties and dangers had passed and a new dawn had come. Hostilities had ended in Europe.

It was now 1945. There had not been a General Election since 1935. Ten years had gone by since an appeal to the electorate. During half of the period there had been a Tory Government, and, in the remaining half, a coalition of the three major Parties. An election during the war, if advisable, was certainly not practicable because of the movement of population, the thousands of men and women in the services, many abroad, and, under these circumstances a general desire for no change.

The ending of the war in Europe brought the three major Parties face to face with the issue of a General Election. Some months before the cessation of hostilities the Prime Minister had stated that, in his opinion, the life of the then Parliament, ten years old by this time, had long exceeded its legal term and should be brought to an end at the earliest possible moment after hostilities with Germany came to an end. Mr Churchill, however, suggested to the leaders of the three Parties the possibility of continuing the coalition until the end of the war with Japan. The response was unfavourable, although they were willing for the coalition to continue until the end of the session in Ocober.

On 18 May, the eve of the Labour Party Conference, Mr Churchill wrote to the three leaders—Labour, Liberal and National Liberal—suggesting the continuance of the coalition until the ending of the war with Japan, and suggested they should discuss means for taking a referendum on the issue. Without distinctly saying so, he gave them to understand, in case of a refusal, he would dissolve Parliament immediately.

At the Labour Party Conference, this proposal was rejected. It was also rejected by the Liberal Party. Mr Ernest Brown, for the National Liberals, said he was willing to continue the coalition until the end of hostilities with Japan. The Party managers of the Tory Party were pressing Mr Churchill for a July election. From the end of the war they took this line, feeling it was favourable, party-wise, for their chances. The three major Parties were favourable to the idea of a General Election and, on 23 May 1945, Mr Churchill laid his resignation before the King, and was immediately requested to form a new Government. This he did and it was called a Caretaker Government. It was short-lived, for he asked for a dissolution of Parliament on 15 June. Polling day was fixed for 5 July 1945. At the dissolution, the House of Commons membership was 358 Tory members, 163 Labour, 26 National Liberals, 18 Liberals, 20 Independents and 23 other Parties.

The Parliament elected in 1935 came to an end. During its long life, long for a Parliament to run, there had been three Prime Ministers: Stanley Baldwin, Neville Chamberlain and Winston Churchill. For half the period it had been an unusual Parliament for there had been changes, not only in Prime Minister but changes in places where it met. There had been little controversy; nevertheless there had been important legislation. This is not to say there was no controversy at all. There certainly was. Some of the debates were very critical and, at question-time for one hour in every sitting day, Ministers were often questioned critically. Recently I have refreshed my memory by reading some of the debates and looking at some of the questions on a variety of topics in both the domestic and the international sphere, and the many matters respecting the conduct of the war in its many aspects and the problems arising from it. All of it provides nostalgic reading, and is a reminder of an unusual period in Parliamentary life. I hope that neither the British Parliament nor the British people will have to pass through and endure such circumstances again.

On a lovely sunny day on 5 July 1945, the General Election took place. The weather was ideal for the occasion. The results of the election were not known for three weeks. The postal votes from electors in the Forces, many of whom were still overseas, were the reason for the delay. On 25 July, the appointed day for the declaration, there was a magnificent, resounding victory for Labour. I was the Labour candidate for the Mansfield constituency—my first contested election. There were two candidates and I was returned with a 28,000 majority.

The new Parliament met on 1 August 1945, and the new House of Commons memberships were Labour 392, Tories 189, Liberals 12, I.L.P. 3, Communists 2, Irish Nationalists 2, and 24 others. It was, as will be observed from this figure, a landslide for the Labour Party, and it was the first time Labour had been able to form a Government with a majority in the House of Commons. On the two previous occasions, 1924 and 1929, when Labour had the larger number of seats, they had not had an overall majority. In some quarters the result of the election was a great surprise. The Tories were of the opinion that with Mr Churchill leading them they would have an easy victory. Even the most optimistic in the Labour Party were surprised at the size of the victory.

The Party went into the campaign with colours flying, with a programme of reform in the social sphere based on the Beveridge Report, and proposals for fundamental changes in the economic field, such as the nationalization of the basic industries. The electorate gave their answer as to the kind of Government they wanted to deal with the problems in the early post-war period.

On the first day of the new Parliament, everyone on the

Government side of the House was elated. There were many new faces; some had retired, some had been defeated, and many were entering the House for the first time. On this first day, there was an unprecedented incident, one that I shall always remember: Mr Churchill, entering the Chamber to take his place on the Opposition front bench, I am sure, naturally disappointed with the result of the election, was greeted by his supporters with the song, 'For he's a jolly good fellow'. They did it lustily and well. As the strains died away, George Griffiths, the member for Hemsworth in South Yorkshire, a miner and member of the Salvation Army, began to sing the 'Red Flag'. It was taken up by the Government supporters, rising to their feet. I had two friends in the public gallery, Miss Isobel Ford and George Jelley, who both enjoyed the scene and the singing. Frequently I see them and often they remark, 'That day in August 1945, in the House of Commons! What an event to remember, and what a privilege to be there to hear the voices and witness order papers waving!' The members of the opposition were discomfited and, I think, regarded the singing of the 'Red Flag' as sacrilege. I doubt that if the Tories had not started the singing it would have happened, although jubilation was great and spirits were high, but I am certain it was neither premeditated nor organized, for it was such a spontaneous outburst, a counterblast to the Tories. I had no idea when I obtained the two tickets for Isobel and George that they were going to witness a scene that had not happened previously.

On this day the names of the Cabinet and Ministerial appointments were known. Mr Attlee, Labour's first Prime Minister with a majority in the House of Commons, had chosen his team, among whom was Jim Griffiths, Minister of National Insurance, with a seat in the Cabinet. He immediately asked me to be his Parliamentary Private Secretary. Such a post has disadvantages as well as advantages, for you are restricted in the House of Commons from asking questions and taking part in debates on matters connected with the department concerned. National Insurance and the implementation of the Beveridge Report and the expansion of the Social Services were going to figure prominently in the Government's legislation. I knew by accepting the invitation I would be restricted so far as the House of Commons was concerned. On the other hand I realized from the experience I had gained in the Union and Local Government that I could be of help to Jim Griffiths and I believe he was of that opinion. On reflection, I have no doubt that my decision to accept the invitation was right. I have no regrets and, during the five years I worked with Jim Griffiths, he afforded me every facility to participate in the work of the Department and I was privileged to be in at the discussions when the legislation was being prepared. I worked with him and enjoyed his confidence at this new created Ministry—the Ministry of National Insurance to which I shall refer in a later chapter.

The war had left its scars. The population was scattered, the Forces personnel were in many parts of the world and there was physical damage in many cities and towns on an extensive scale. This combination of circumstances caused by the war created many problems and the financial situation was unsound. The nation's treasure had been poured out during the six years at war. Mr Churchill was reported as saying that the nation would be bankrupt at the end of the war.

The first post-war Government in 1945 faced a considerable task: the repair of physical damage with many houses and homes destroyed, and many that were not habitable; the rebuilding of the economy; better and more adequate social provision for those who were old, sick and injured. In my twenty-five years' experience in the House of Commons, no Parliament worked harder and longer than the one from 1945 to 1950 when the first post-war Parliament came to an end. A catalogue of the legislation in the economic and social field would indicate the vast amount of work that was done in the legislative and administrative sphere, and the changes that took place, some of which today are taken for granted, were started only twenty-five years ago.

One memory I still retain was the nationalization of the coal industry. The Bill was introduced into the House of Commons by Emmanuel Shinwell. It passed through the House on its Second Reading and, after a prolonged Committee stage with opposition from the Tory members, it finally reached its Third Reading. At the end of the debate, a division took place, for it was strenuously opposed by the Opposition, as was expected. It was the first blow against the citadel of private ownership in industry. Here was a clash of ideologies, and it was fought to the last ditch. Going through the aye lobby in the crowd, the Welsh part of the miners' group, in a mood of triumph, burst into song. 'Cwm Rhondda' was the tune and the strains of 'Songs of Praises I will give ever to thee' rang out of that division lobby. Everyone took part. Indeed it was a moment of jubilation. It is not the experience of all who have been propagandists and have agitated for changes to see their dreams become realities. Many in the division that day, including myself, had agitated and argued for nationalization. In the Union Lodge meetings, it was not difficult to do this among miners. The majority of them had voted for it, for among other things it was advocated by the Labour Party at the election. For many years, men of my generation, not only at Branch meetings but in the open air and in market squares had advocated nationalization, and also at Commissions, Royal and ordinary, the most notable being the Sankey Commission of 1919 where Bob Smillie, the miners' President, reasoned the case for nationalization. Twenty-five years later the day had come. It was a memorable one and the opening of a new chapter in what was, at that time, Britain's basic industry.

In the 1945 Parliament, there were so many changes taking place that it would require volumes to record it all. For me they provide nostalgic memories.

India was very much under discussion during the 1945 Parliament. It was a country administered by Britain from 1858. It was a troubled country, with planned civil disobedience. Although there was bitter dissension between the two main political parties, the Hindus and the Muslims, they were both agreed on one thing, the desire to be rid of Whitehall control. In 1945 a good-will mission was sent out to India consisting of Pethwick Lawrence, M.P. who was Secretary of State for India, A. V. Alexander, First Lord of the Admiralty, and Sir Stafford Cripps, President of the Board of Trade. When they returned to England, they stressed the importance of early political action to meet a situation fraught with grave danger. Mr Attlee was convinced that when she became independent India would find great advantages in remaining within the Commonwealth. He made it clear that the choice must be her own, and that, if she elected to go outside, it would be for Britain to assist the transition. This assurance that no obstacle would be placed in the way of complete independence was welcomed in India.

India was a real problem because the Hindus and Muslims could not agree on the unity of India but Mr Attlee, in introducing the India Independence Bill on 10 July 1947, said, 'Delay will jeopardize success'. In the Bill the Indian people, through their representatives, were given the opportunity of deciding on the division of territory. It is a long story and, though I do not pretend to be knowledgeable on Indian matters, I was impressed by the situation in India as told to the House by the Prime Minister and by his anxiety to give Independence to India. Among many things Mr Attlee said during the debate was: 'This Bill brings to an end one chapter in the long connection between Britain and India but it opens another. British rule, which has endured so long now at the instance of this country, is coming to an end.' Concluding his speech he expressed the wish that they, the Indians, would long remain with Britain, and that the friendship which united so many British and Indians, despite all the strains of recent years, would continue and extend even more widely. It was a great step forward in decolonization, a process of change, in which millions of people in India and, later on, in Asia and Africa, were liberated and given the opportunity of governing themselves. The giving of Independence to India was, at that time, and remains, a bright jewel in the crown of the Prime Minister. Decolonization has accelerated and now there is the Commonwealth in which partnership has taken the place of exploitation.

The 1945 Parliament was a memorable one. It was the beginning of a peaceful revolution, a period of change in our history, in the economic, social and colonial spheres. Twenty per cent of the economy became public undertakings; the foundations of the Welfare State were laid, and decolonization was speeded up. They were great and exciting days to my colleagues and myself who supported the Government. The greater part of my time was taken up at the Ministry of National Insurance. When there was little likelihood of any divisions in the House of Commons, which was not often, we would be there later in the evening, and, when there was the possibility of division, which was most sitting days because the legislation was controversial, the Minister had a room in the House. I remember even now the number—forty-five. That room where so much of the Department's work was done is now part of the cafeteria.

In 1950 the first post-war Parliament was dissolved and the Prime Minister, a few months before the statutory limit of five years, decided on a General Election. It was back to another campaign and activities of a kind different from those of the previous five years. Those of us who had supported the Government were proud of what had been done, not that all the early post-war difficulties had been overcome, but the tasks undertaken had been enormous. There was so much on the credit side. The Labour Party was full of confidence. One thing was sure: the trust placed in the Labour Government had not been misplaced. But, the result of the 1950 Election was disappointing. It would be wrong not to admit this. The majority in the House of Commons was considerably reduced, to six. However, this was sufficient to enable Mr Attlee to form a Government for the second time.

The continuation of food rationing was an irritation; it had been in operation for the six-year period of the war. It was now 1950 and, in the view of the Government, in order to ensure a policy of 'fair shares', it was not possible to abandon the coupon book. With the best will in the world, to abolish rationing whilst shortages existed would have meant rationing by the size of the purse. The propaganda of the Tories and allied organizations was intense on this particular issue and was not free from malice and bitterness. My own view was that this particular issue must have made an impact on the electorate. The propaganda of the Tories and the Housewives' League had not been unsuccessful. It is one of the circumstances of political life that you have to live with, prepare for and combat sometimes success, sometimes failure.

I was again the Labour candidate for Mansfield. This time there were four candidates : Socialist, Tory, Liberal and Communist. One thing I noticed: the numbers attending the meetings had declined despite similar arrangements made as in 1945 and previous elections. The idea was to visit each area at least twice but at all the places there was a decline in numbers. It was a little mystifying at the time but it has happened at every succeeding election and is general throughout the country. In 1950 the television media was growing and this process continues. You hear such remarks as 'Well, I can sit at home and look and listen. There is no need to attend meetings.' Television has given a mortal blow to attendances at political meetings during elections. A lot of the spice and humour and atmosphere has gone, and I doubt whether election meetings will ever again be the magnet they were prior to 1950. New techniques have been devised : loud speakers in the streets, more effective use of hoardings, visits to factory gates and, where permission is obtained, attendance at works' canteens. Referring to early post-war problems, I recall one meeting where a man in the audience produced from a box a quantity of stone and foreign matter that he had received with his coal. He protested that he was paying for muck that would not burn. He blamed the miners for it. I was informed of the man's political affiliations and that this was his particular stick with which to beat the Government. What he did not understand was that, during and after the war, because coal was in such demand, there being a coal famine, new machines to increase coal production were being used, and the cleaning and washing process had been neglected.

I recall going to Rugby during the 1945 election. Ronald Lewis, now the member for Carlisle, was the candidate. It was a packed meeting. I said, 'I am a miner from Mansfield. I have heard of Rugby and its public school. You good people may have heard of coal miners. May I say this? Miners are neither saints nor devils, have neither horns nor wings, but one thing they do not do is to vote Tory at election time. The Mansfield constituency, at no election in its history, has returned a Tory to the House of Commons.' It went down well and brought the audience in uproar with laughter.

I was returned at the 1950 election with a handsome

majority of 24,000. With such a small majority in the House of Commons, the Parliamentary situation was precarious and all members wondered how long the Government could last. However, Mr Attlee was able and did form another Government. There were Ministerial changes: James Griffiths was made Colonial Secretary and was succeeded by Dr Edith Summerskill as Minister of National Insurance. Before the opening of the new Parliament and my return to London, I had a telephone message calling me to 10, Downing Street. It was during the morning and I was able to make the journey to London the same day and arrive reasonably early. On arrival at Number Ten, I was shown into the Cabinet Room where Mr Attlee sat busy with papers. The conversation was brief. He told me of the change at the Ministry of National Insurance and said he would like me to be Parliamentary Secretary. He referred to my experience and work as Parliamentary Private Secretary to James Griffiths. He said he was appreciative of the work I had done. He said I must have gained extensive knowledge at the Department and also from the legislation that had gone through Parliament and were now Acts of Parliament. I was pleased to accept the appointment, and so began a new chapter as a Junior Minister to Dr Edith Summerskill.

The interview lasted about ten minutes. Mr Attlee certainly did not waste his words which were short, crisp and sharp. He came to the point straightaway. This was his usual manner in the House of Commons. At the despatch box, answering questions or taking part in debates, he adopted the same attitude, with nothing extravagant or flamboyant but just clear and concise language. I recall that during the second reading of the India Independence Bill, Mr Attlee opened the debate and, at the beginning, he apologized to the House saying that he would speak longer than was his usual custom.

My first visit to the Cabinet Room was so brief that I had not the opportunity for a good look round but I did, in imagination, visualize circumstances and people who had graced the room where many historic decisions had been made. The Prime Minister wished me good luck and expressed the hope that I would be happy. The all too brief stay I shall refer to in a later chapter about the Ministry of National Insurance.

The 1950 Parliament was short-lived—only eighteen months—for in 1951 the Prime Minister called a General Election. Circumstances were difficult: only a small majority and differences in the Cabinet over charges for some of the services in the Health Services, such as prescription charges, dental and opthalmic appliances. This caused a rumpus and unpleasant divisions in the Government and the Parliamentary Labour Party. There were resignations by Aneurin Bevan, Harold Wilson and John Freeman, all Ministers. They considered that these proposals were wrong and could be the beginning of the erosion of the National Health Service and that, if the Tories came back to power, this could be regarded as a dangerous precedent. Certainly succeeding Governments have used this as a precedent for attacks on the Health Service. The original idea of Beveridge and the legislation introduced by Aneurin Bevan, who was Minister of Health in the 1945 Government, was that the whole cost of the Health Services should be a charge on the National Exchequer, apart from the weekly contribution of National Insurance contributors by employers, employees and the self-employed. 1951 was the beginning of a difficult decade for the Parliamentary Party. The cohesion and unity of the 1945 Parliament was weakened by these resignations, and these circumstances had repercussions in the constituencies. With the small majority of six and with difficulties inside the Party, the 1950 Parliament was of short duration—only eighteen months.

I was again the Labour candidate for Mansfield. This time the field of runners was confined to two—Labour and Tory. Boundary changes had been effected, reducing the size of the electorate and the area. Mansfield Woodhouse and Blidworth had become part of the Newark constituency. Because of this change, my majority was reduced but was still a handsome one of 21,000. The taking of Mansfield Woodhouse out of the Mansfield constituency was a mistake. I said this at the Inquiry that was held on the matter. Blidworth was a different proposition. It was at the eastern end of the constituency and for local government purposes was part of the Southwell Rural

District Council, the whole area being in the Newark constituency with Blidworth the exception. Although Blidworth had been a part of the Mansfield constituency from its inception in 1885, the case for its becoming part of Newark was unanswerable. There was, however, one consolation in the change. Newark was won for Labour and my good friend and colleague, George Deer, became the first Labour Member of Parliament for the Newark constituency.

The election of 1951 resulted in a change of Government. The Tories won and, for the first time in peacetime, Mr Churchill became Prime Minister. He had been in politics and in the House of Commons for many years in Liberal and Tory Governments. He had held many Ministerial positions. For many years in the political wilderness, the day had at last dawned for him. He had won his first election as Leader of the Tory Party to become Prime Minister for the first time, because in the period of the war he had been chosen with the consent and approval of the three political Parties in Parliament to succeed Mr Neville Chamberlain.

It was the beginning of successive Tory Governments which continued for thirteen years. The new Prime Minister was now seventy-five years old but still vigorous and, in 1951, showed little, if any, sign of physical and mental inability, having recovered from the disappointment of the 1945 Election. The electoral success of 1951 was a tonic to him and, with his natural pugnacity and determination, he carried on as Prime Minister until 1955.

The first meeting of the new Parliament in 1951 meant a crossing of the floor of the House for the Labour members. Instead of occupying the benches on the right of the Speaker as the Government and its supporters do, now, as the Opposition, they sat on his left. The Tories were as jubilant, having won the election, as Labour had been in 1945. The electors had given their verdict; Demos had spoken and we had a Tory Government.

One piece of legislation I remember so well in this Parliament was the Mines' and Quarries' Bill of 1954. This was about safety, health and welfare in these industries. Apart from regulation making orders there had been no major mining legislation for forty years—a long time. But circumstances had changed. New techniques in the industry were being applied and mechanization was taking place, and this was a sphere where a fresh look was urgently needed and for which the Miners' Federation had been pressing. It was a coincidence that the Prime Minister, Mr Churchill, when President of the Board of Trade in the Liberal Government of 1911, had introduced the Coal Mines' Bill in the House of Commons. The Bill of 1954 was a lengthy one. After the Second Reading, months were passed while the Standing Committee scrutinized the Bill.

A number of the Miners' group, of which I was one, played a prominent part in the discussions : Bill Blyton, a miner from Durham, Harold Neal from the Derbyshire coal-field, Harold Finch from South Wales, Ronnie Williams, the Miners' Federation legal adviser and Member of Parliament for Wigan, and others whose names escape me now. They all did a great job and the practical knowledge they had and the detailed study that was given to the Bill made the Committee stage interesting. The aim of everyone was to produce an Act of Parliament to meet the need in the changed and changing circumstances of mining practice : the greatest possible measures of safety, and the health and welfare of all those who work in this most dangerous and hazardous mining and quarrying industry.

During the Third Reading (the final stage before becoming an Act of Parliament) in which I took part, I said the Bill contained many important provisions like ventilation, gas accumulation, prevention of fire and the height of roadways. In the Bill, on the Second Reading, a minimum height of five feet was proposed. We tried unsuccessfully to obtain a minimum height of six feet. The Minister, Geoffrey Lloyd, met us half way with five feet six inches. I expressed the hope that mining practice in future would be to make roadways higher than the minimum of five feet six. I also, on the Third Reading, made a reference to the Inspectorate in the Nottinghamshire coal-field. Numerically, it was below standard. After all, the Inspectorate of Mines are the watchdogs of the statutory mining safety regulations. My concluding words were : 'It is my hope that what has been done during the past few months in committee, seeking to improve the Bill, that its provisions will reflect itself in a reduction of fatal and non-fatal accidents, and the number of victims of industrial disease.' To achieve this a co-operative effort by the National Coalboard, the National Union of Mineworkers and each individual workman was necessary and important.

In 1955 there was another General Election. I was again the Labour candidate for the Mansfield constituency—my fifth successive contest. I had been in Parliament now for sixteen years. There had been many changes in personnel. This happens at every election, for there are retirements, members are defeated and after an election many new faces appear in the House. The Mansfield constituency was again re-distributed for this Election. Mansfield Woodhouse came back, but Sutton-in-Ashfield was taken out to form a new constituency to be called the Ashfield division. Warsop, which was part of the Bassetlaw division, was brought into the Mansfield constituency. My reduced electorate nett was 20,000. There were again only two candidates, a Tory and myself. My majority of 16,000 was still substantial in spite of the reduced electorate. The Tories again won and formed a Government with Mr Churchill as Prime Minister. In the 1950s the Labour movement had many losses. Deaths and retirements took their toll; Stafford Cripps, Arthur Greenwood and Ernest Bevin had died; Clement Attlee had given up the leadership; Hugh Dalton had retired. These men, whose names were universally known, were all men of stature and had stamped their image on Parliamentary life. They will long be remembered by my generation, and will have a page in history. In the contest for the leadership, Hugh Gaitskill was elected, greatly to the disappointment of Herbert Morrison who eventually went to the Lords.

Mr Churchill, after the 1955 election, did not stay long as Prime Minister. He was feeling the weight of his years, for by this time he was eighty. He was succeeded as Prime Minister by Sir Anthony Eden. But very shortly after his accession came the Suez Affair. I would think the scenes in the House of Commons were unprecedented. There was uproar. The Prime

Minister and the Foreign Secretary, Mr Selwyn Lloyd, had a very rough time. There were occasions when the Speaker suspended the sittings. The atmosphere was electric. There were moments when the place was bedlam with more members on their feet at the same time wanting to speak, than I had, at any one time, witnessed. There were Ministerial resignations over the issue. Sir Edward Boyle and Mr Anthony Nutting, who were in disagreement over the issue, left the Government as a protest. I recall the speech of Aneurin Bevan, perhaps one of his best orations during his long Parliamentary career; it is on the record in Hansard, but to have heard it in the prevalent atmosphere was memorable.

The Suez episode left its mark on the Prime Minister. He became ill and resigned not only the Premiership but his seat in Parliament. He accepted a Peerage and is now known as Lord Avon. Who was to be his successor? Who was to restore the fortunes of the Tory Party not only at home, where they were not good, but abroad, particularly in the United States of America which had strongly disapproved of Britain's part in the Suez affair? There were plenty of guesses at Westminster. The majority of members speculated that the choice would be Mr R. A. Butler. He was, however, in the shadows and, when the news broke that Mr Harold Macmillan was to be Prime Minister, there was surprise in the corridors at Westminster. He formed his new Government which carried on until 1959, when Parliament was dissolved and a General Election was held with Mr Macmillan leading the Tories and Hugh Gaitskill the Labour Party.

At this election I was again the Labour candidate in Mansfield. There were again only two candidates in Mansfield, a Tory and myself. I was re-elected with a 16,000 majority. The Tories won this election, the third in succession, and Mr Macmillan, as Prime Minister, formed the new Government.

A few months after the election of 1959, Aneurin Bevan was taken ill. It turned out to be a mortal illness, and in the middle of the following year he died. Soon afterwards Hugh Gaitskill died. The loss of these two, Leader and Deputy Leader of the Labour Party, was shattering. It was not only a great loss to the Labour Party, but also to Parliament. They

F

came from different backgrounds, one, Aneurin Bevan, from the pits, the other, Hugh Gaitskill, from the University, with a brilliant academic background. They had different temperaments and approaches to problems which often led to differences, often clashes, but it was more about means than ends. It was sad and tragic that Parliament and the nation should have lost the ability and talent of them both when they were comparatively young and could have served Parliament and the nation for a number of years.

In this period, Sir Winston Churchill was still in Parliament. He had been a successful candidate at the 1959 elections and, in spite of his years, attended the House frequently. He certainly loved the House of Commons but now age and physical impairment was very much in evidence and he seldom employed his skill and long experience in Parliamentary debates. Many to whom I have referred had either died or retired or had accepted Peerages and were now in the House of Lords whose members were either hereditary Peers of first creation or from a long line of succession.

In this period, 1958, I believe it was, Lord Stansgate better known as Mr Wedgwood Benn, died. For many years prior to his acceptance of a Peerage he had been a Member of the House of Commons. As a Peer, his eldest son, Tony Wedgwood Benn succeeded him. He was returned by one of the Bristol constituencies to succeed Sir Stafford Cripps in the House of Commons. As the eldest son, succeeding to his father's title, he was disfranchised from sitting in the House of Commons. He refused to take his seat in the House of Lords and was determined to fight, and so he did. When the by-election took place to fill the vacancy caused by his disfranchisement, he was one of the candidates and was successful, but he was still not permitted to take his seat in the House of Commons. What a dilemma it was for the Government and Parliament, a unique and unprecedented situation! Were the electors in the Bristol constituency to be disfranchised and not have a Member of Parliament? These circumstances were the prelude to a constitutional change, the outcome of which was a Bill presented to Parliament permitting Peers to renounce their titles and their rights to sit in the House of Lords as the eldest sons of their fathers, and to become eligible to sit in the House of Commons. The 1958 Bill provided for the creation of Life Peers. Tony Wedgwood Benn persisted with a dogged determination and won the day, and brought about a constitutional change which altered the composition of the House of Lords. In 1963, Harold Macmillan, the Prime Minister, decided to leave Parliament. There was no election—not yet. Parliament could go on another year before the statutory limit of five years had arrived. The Foreign Secretary, the Earl of Home, was chosen by the Tory Party to succeed Harold Macmillan as Prime Minister. The Earl of Home took advantage of the provisions of the Peerage Act (1963) to renounce his title, and make himself available for a seat in the House of Commons. Mr R. A. Butler, in the shadows as in 1956, was again passed over. Had it not been for the Life Peerage's Act, enabling the Earl of Home to renounce his seat in the Lords, would the choice have been Mr Butler? Who knows? There was a by-election in the Scottish constituency of Perth and Kinross. Sir Alec Douglas-Home, as he now was, won the election and became Prime Minister, but only for a few months until the election of 1964.

The 1959 Parliament went on to the last moment. It is worth noting that between 1951 and 1964, there had been four Prime Ministers. I recall that during the summer of 1963, when the recess was extended for two weeks, while the Perth and Kinross election was taking place, I met an old friend in Mansfield who was a member of the clerical profession. He remarked, 'An extra two weeks' recess, I notice! Is this on account of the by-election? Tell me, Mr Taylor, who is going to win?' I remarked, 'Are the days of miracles passed?' 'Certainly not, Mr Taylor,' he replied. 'In that event,' I said, 'the Labour candidate could win but, if he did win, I would regard it a miracle.' He did not win and, when Parliament met in October 1963, Sir Alec Douglas-Home was back in the House of Commons, not as a back-bencher as the Member for Lanark, but as Prime Minister.

With the untimely and unexpected death of Hugh Gaitskill in 1961, the two contestants for the leadership of the Labour Party were Harold Wilson and George Brown. The former emerged as the successful one in the ballot, the latter becoming Deputy Leader. This issue being settled, the great need was to consolidate and secure maximum unity, and to forget the dissensions of the past few years, for on the near horizon was an impending General Election. Preparation and consolidation were the aim, for, at the latest, the election had to take place in 1964. There were many speculations and rumours as to how long the Prime Minister would carry on. One of his compatriots, Sir Harry Lauder, used to sing 'Keep right on to the end of the road'. Sir Alec, the Prime Minister, did this all right. He went on to the end of the statutory limit of five years before dissolving Parliament.

The election was held in 1964. I was again the candidate for the Mansfield constituency. On this occasion there were four candidates—Tory, Liberal, Communist and Labour. I was again elected with a handsome majority. The national result was close, with Labour successful with a majority of three, too close to be comfortable. Even with so small a margin, however, a Labour Government was possible and Harold Wilson became Prime Minister. On each occasion when a division took place members would wait anxiously for the result. Would the Government survive was the question! It was on everyone's lips. But survive it did, though only for eighteen months, at which time the Prime Minister sought a dissolution and called for a General Election. It was a precarious position, a knife-edge, every time a division in the House took place. I recall that two months after the 1964 Election, I developed a hernia and was medically advised to have surgical treatment. I approached the Chief Whip on this. He asked if I could postpone entering hospital until another Member who was recuperating from an illness was able to return to the House.

This was the situation in the 1964 Parliament. Whenever there was a division in the House of Commons, every Member was required and expected to be there. My good friend, Sir John Nicolson the surgeon, now deceased, who was sympathetic to the Labour Movement and the Government, said to me: 'If you are needed and everything is all right after the first few days, we will take you by ambulance to the House, for if you are within the precincts of the House of Commons your vote can be recorded.' This happened on many occasions during the 1950-1 Parliament. Members who were under the care of Sir John were brought from the Manor House Hospital in North London to record their vote. As in 1950, with a majority of six, so in the 1964 Parliament, every member supporting the Government was, if at all possible, expected by the Chief Whip to be there, for the fate of the Government depended upon his vote.

The autumn of 1965 came and I was now seventy years of age. I decided, and publicly announced, that this would be my last Parliament. With such a small majority it was uncertain and anybody's guess, how long Parliament would last. The election could come quickly; on the other hand the Government could carry on, having survived for twelve months under difficult circumstances.

In view of the uncertainty it was important for the constituency to have time to put the machinery in motion to appoint my successor. The election came in April 1966, only five months after I had announced my retirement, and not too long a time to appoint a candidate.

After twenty-five years in the House of Commons, having been the Member for Mansfield for a longer period than any of my predecessors, I said 'Goodbye' to the House of Commons, with regret and sadness. It had been a wonderful experience. At the lowering of the curtain I was confirmed in my opinion that it was a privilege to be a Member of Parliament. I can only hope that it may be recorded that I served the constituency well, as did my predecessors in the eighty years from the birth of the constituency in 1885, in making a contribution towards advancing the welfare of the people, supporting a greater measure of social justice and in making an advance along the road to Socialism. For the experience I shall be ever grateful. It enriched my life with memories of events, the many people I met and the opportunities of visiting other countries.

In the days of my youth the last thought in my mind was that I should one day be a Member of the House of Commons. Behind that door in the pit, in the dark, now sixty-one years

ago, I imagined many things, but never that I should be a
Member of Parliament. My Sunday School teacher often said,
'The future is wisely hidden from us.'

Although it was a rich and satisfying experience, I had many
ups and down: moments of frustration but also moments of
elation. I am pleased to say that there were more of the latter
when I was able, by virtue of being a Member of Parliament,
to help someone with his or her problems, and by Ministerial
action and Parliamentary means, furnish a solution to a problem and give satisfaction. Writing from memory, I have related
experiences and events as they have come bubbling up. Much
I have not put down but I must mention the humour of the
House of Commons of which there is plenty. I give just one
example. There was a Member whose speeches were always
typed and had all the punctuations and exclamation marks put
in; in one speech he came to a part where he said, 'Mr Speaker,
at this stage, I would like to ask myself a question.' The
Speaker, Captain Fitzroy, was heard to mutter, inaudibly he
thought (maybe he was thinking the speech was becoming too
long), 'And a fine answer you will get!' The House rocked with
laughter, but the Member went on, undaunted. Maybe he was
unaware of what the Speaker had said!

CHAPTER XII

National Insurance

The Ministry of National Insurance was a newly created Government Department. It was the child of the Act of 1944 made during the latter days of the wartime coalition. The first Minister was Sir William Jowitt, K.C., M.P., who held this office for a few months only. When the coalition ended in 1945 he was succeeded by Mr Hore-Belisha, M.P. during the period of the Caretaker Government, which was a few weeks only. From its creation to the General Election of 1945 the Department's work was rather more prospective than actual. In the days immediately following the election, the scene began to change and the headquarters of the Department, situated in Carlton House Terrace, facing the Mall and opposite St James's Park, became a hive of industry and activity. The vacant Ministerial chair was occupied by James Griffiths, M.P., and George Lindgren, M.P. who had been successful at Wellingborough at the election, became Parliamentary Secretary. Both these appointments were made by the Prime Minister, Mr Attlee.

There was a practice and custom, which continues to be part of Parliamentary life, for a Minister to have a Parliamentary Private Secretary, the choice being made by the Minister himself. As I have said, Jim Griffiths asked me to undertake this duty and I accepted. Although such a post placed restrictions upon one in Parliament itself, it had compensating advantages. To be in the confidence of a Minister like Jim Griffiths and to take part in the discussions was a wonderful experience.

When I arrived at Carlton House Terrace the machinery for the task ahead was being activated. There was important work to be done in the legislative and administrative spheres. The few who were at the Department, and they were small in number at the time, had no illusions about the task in front of them. It was realized by all, including the Civil Service, that the legislative and administrative aspects were complementary. The former was of no value without an efficient administration. Both sides of the coin had to be seen and the magnitude of the job was apparent to everyone in the Department. Three I remember quite well: firstly Sir Tom Phillips, who had been at the Ministry of Labour. He was a shrewd, quiet and unassuming man, so wise and helpful for the task that lay ahead. No Minister could have been better served by a Permanent Secretary. Then there were Sir Henry Hancock from the Ministry of Food who was Deputy Secretary, and Mr McCartney, the Minister's Private Secretry. These three were most helpful with their advice and were in the best traditions of the British Civil Service.

What was the task? The implementation of the Beveridge Report. As part of this, the Ministry of National Insurance was to be responsible for the administration of the Family Allowances' Act. The fixing of the appointed day for its implementation was arranged quickly and was to be in August 1946. For this, the administrative machine began to function. There were teething troubles initially, but these were overcome and the difficulties were soon resolved. Books had to be printed and application forms, supplying the information, had to be returned—all matters demanding the immediate attention of the newly recruited staff who were centred at Blackpool under the supervision of Mr Driver. Eventually matters began to work smoothly in this new administrative field.

As soon as we assumed office we also had the task of preparing the legislation to implement the Beveridge Report. Members of the House of Commons, particularly the Government supporters, were asking and pressing for speed in bringing in the Bills to implement it. The first problems to be tackled were the proposals and legislation in the sphere of industrial accidents and occupational disease. The Bill was to be called, and is known throughout industry as the Industrial

Injuries' Act. The main feature of the Bill was to replace the Workmen's Compensation Acts which began in 1897.

The second job was to replace the Health Insurance scheme begun by Lloyd George in 1912, and to institute a system of National Insurance on a universal scale for the elderly, the sick and widows. The other parts of the Beveridge plan, the creation of a National Health Service, and a system of National Assistance were undertaken by the Ministry of Health whose Minister was Aneurin Bevan. The whole of this legislation was prepared and passed through all its Parliamentary stages, and the day appointed for it all to operate was 5 July 1948. I, and many others, regard this day as a landmark in Britain's social history.

My own interest was immense, particularly in the sphere of industrial accidents and occupational diseases. The experience of Jim Griffiths and myself was identical as coal-miners. For many years we had worked underground, and we had witnessed so much—particularly both fatal and non-fatal accidents to individuals. They were daily occurrences but got little publicity as they were known only to those in the area where they happened. We often talked of disasters that had shaken the nation : Sengenydd, Gresford and Whitehaven where there were hundreds of unfortunate victims and dependents numbering thousands. We were also aware of the thousands of less serious accidents, and the growth of occupational diseases particularly pneumoconiosis, all of which involved compensation.

For many years there had been an unsatisfactory state of affairs especially in those industries with a high incidence of accident and disease. There were many difficulties and problems. For example, payments were geared to earnings and not to the degree of disability. Also there was the vexed question : did the accident or disease arise out of, and in the course of, the employment? The onus of proving this was on the workman. Those dealing with these matters knew only too well how vexatious and troublesome they were and how they were the root cause of dissatisfaction. All this was recognized by the Beveridge Report and the time was ripe for change. A common, almost daily, expression among the miners and the

Union was that for decades Workmen's compensation had been a hunting ground for the legal and medical professions. If the amount of fees and money spent by Trade Unions and employers to establish or refute a claim could be known, the size of it would be astounding.

The purpose of the Industrial Injuries' legislation was to replace the Workmen's Compensation Acts and make other, and better, provisions on behalf of those who were to have the misfortune to be injured at work or contract one of the recognized industrial diseases. After 5 July 1948 the old Workmen's Compensation would be replaced by a system, the main feature of which would be that benefit payments would be governed by the degree of disability, with no reference to pre-accident earnings. The administration, settling and deciding entitlemnt to benefit, was to be in the hands of the Ministry of National Insurance. In case of dispute between the Ministry and the injured person, the matter would be settled by a tribunal with no recourse to litigation and the courts. The liability for payment of benefit would be transferred from the employers and the insurance companies to an Industrial Injuries' Fund to which the employers and employees and the National Exchequer would contribute. Since the Act there have been fewer arguments about disputed claims and less litigation, and my experience is that it has worked well. Moreover, the Act, in my judgement, was a silent revolution, a new venture and an entirely fresh approach in this sphere of human tragedy—for tragedy it is for a person to be the victim of accident and disease. In one moment he is deprived of his faculty to earn a livelihood and robbed of the opportunity to enjoy life, and there are many such people in industry. What a tragedy it is to leave home fit and well and full of spirit and hope for the future and in a moment to be disabled for life.

Another aspect of industrial life is worthy of mention. I regard it of great importance, and it has certainly brought financial benefit to injured workmen. I have often wondered whether the significance and importance have been fully understood. I refer to the 'Doctrine of Common Employment'. By a Court decision almost a century before 1945 it was made difficult for an employee to be successful in a claim for damages at Common Law if the employer's negligence caused the accident. In many of the cases it would have been easy to prove negligence, but the workman had to decide whether he was going to claim compensation or sue for damages. He could not have both. This was a hard choice to make. What made it difficult was that, although it was not difficult to establish negligence, the employer could plead Common Employment and place the liability on the employee responsible for the negligence. This was a much stiffer hurdle than establishing negligence. It was little use taking action against a person whose financial resources were negligible. There were few cases for damages arising through accidents at work up to 1948. The ancient right to damages for accidents at work caused by negligence was of little value because of the existence of Common Employment. The Monkton Committee, under the chairmanship of Sir Walter Monkton, K.C., was set up by the Minister to investigate the question of Common Employment. When the report was published, the majority recommended the abolition of Common Employment, which the Minister accepted. There was a minority report of one signed by Mr Guy De Warren. He was the Secretary of the Midland Coalowners' Association Indemnity Company. He argued for the retention of Common Employment. The change implementing the majority report took place on 5 July 1948. Common Employment, a disadvantageous relic of the past, disappeared and the financial benefit of the change to injured workpeople was enormous. If statistics were available as to the number of successful claims for damages since 1948 and the amount involved, they would tell their own story, and reveal the importance and justification of the step taken in 1948 in the interests of workmen injured at work.

I recall one outstanding example. It was the Creswell colliery disaster in 1951. At the time I was Parliamentary Secretary to the Ministry of National Insurance. I visited the colliery which was only ten miles from my home. Eighty lives were lost. On the evidence of the official enquiry the Miners' Union was satisfied that there was a case for damages. A claim was made by the Nottinghamshire Area of the National Union of Mineworkers. The National Coal Board accepted liability for negligence and the sum of money agreed between the parties, without going to court, was £238,000, available for the dependents of those who had lost their lives. When this was reported to the delegate meeting of the Union, I recall saying to them that had Common Employment not been abolished, three years before the tragedy, it would have been difficult for a claim for damages to have succeeded.

There was a provision in the Bill that in an industry where the employer and the employees agreed, they could have a supplementary scheme providing additional benefit to that provided by the Industrial Injuries' legislation, financed and administered by themselves. The only industry from 1948 to 1970 to take advantage of the provision has been the coal-mining industry. It is a scheme operated by the National Coal Board and the Miners' Union, financed and administered jointly, and it has been of great benefit to injured miners during the past twenty-two years.

The National Insurance legislation, as distinct from the Industrial Injuries' legislation, provided benefit at the time when earnings were interrupted by sickness, unemployment and retirement, and made provision for widowhood, maternity and death grants. Its proposals covered life from the cradle to the grave. It was a big extension of the legislation that existed prior to 1948. Its proposals were universal and covered the whole population. Prior to 1948 there were sections of the community who were outside the existing schemes. Whether you were in or out depended on how much you earned, and the nature of your employment. The National Insurance Act brought everyone in the community under its umbrella. It was universal in its application. It was the beginning of making better and more adequate provision in the form of cash benefits for those whose earnings had been cut off, and who had fallen on hard times as a consequence.

At that time it was bold in concept, and designed to be humane and personal in its administration. Applicants, many of whom had problems, were to be treated as people, not as numbers on a card. The estimated requirements for administrative purposes were a thousand local offices to be staffed and furnished ready for the appointed day in 1948. This was a gigantic task, made more difficult by the legacy of the war, and the shortage of labour, materials and premises.

The task in Mansfield, where the main office for a prescribed area was to be, was not easy. I recall scouring the town for suitable and available premises with Mr McKellar, the Regional Controller. After some difficulty, the Methodist schoolroom in Bridge Street was found available for renting, and this became the first National Insurance Office in Mansfield. It was opened as such on 5 July 1948.

It was not easy to obtain staff for a thousand offices, either for those in the big cities and towns or for the much smaller ones in remote areas. The whole country was included from the Shetlands in the extreme north, to the most southerly parts of Cornwall. The idea was to bring the administration as near as possible to the people, all of whom would be affected. In the provision of staff for these local offices, there were transfers from other Government Departments and from the County Council and County Borough Staff of the Public Assistance Committee.

Also the Friendly Societies and some insurance companies, such as the Prudential and the Refuge, who had been the administrators of the benefit-claim side of the National Health Scheme since it began in 1912. The latter was better known as the Lloyd George Scheme. I say this because in our mining area of Nottinghamshire, you would enquire of someone, 'Aren't you well? Off work?' 'Aye,' the reply would be, 'the doctor has put me on Lloyd George.' This phrase is seldom heard now. Now it's, 'I'm on National Insurance.' The next change is likely to be 'I'm on Social Security' for the name of the Department is the Ministry of Health and Social Security.

The staff were not necessarily local and they included established civil servants from the local government service and new recruits. With crossed fingers and journeying hopefully from the beginning of building the administration, every one of us at Carlton House Terrace had our own private thoughts on the appointed day. At first it seemed a long way off—three years, then two years and then the final lap of one year and there was still so much to do. The Controllers in the regions did splendid jobs in acquiring premises. Their collective effort was rewarded and the whole country was covered on time. I must mention in this connection, one of the Under Secretaries at Carlton House, a man called Mr Rhodes, who was responsible to the Minister for the scheme to be ready on time. Before his death he wrote a pamphlet, 'Setting Up a New Government Department', on the building up of a new government department from scratch. For those who are particularly interested in administration it is well worth reading.

On the appointed day, 5 July 1948, there was jubilation at Carlton House Terrace that so much had been accomplished. From a skeleton of a department in 1945 with a mere handful of people, there were by July 1948 a thousand offices dealing with twenty-three million contributors to the new scheme, and there were hundreds of thousands of claims for different cash benefits. There were of course teething troubles at the beginning. Some of the local offices did better than others but, as experience grew, the administration settled down and began to work smoothly. To have been identified with this venture in the expansion of the Social Services from the beginning was a great and wonderful experience.

When the premises were acquired for the local offices and became staffed the Minister asked me to undertake the job of visiting them. Between 1947 and 1950, prior to becoming Parliamentary Secretary, I visited 300 of the local offices, in every county of England, and many in Wales and Scotland, including some in the Shetlands and Orkneys. I went to the offices taking the good wishes of the Minister, and forging a link between headquarters and the staff. I told them how important the personal touch was and the need for patience and kindness in dealing with the many problems that would be personal in character. The people coming to the office would be the elderly, the sick, the widowed, the injured and disabled people in trouble and difficulties. I believe the Ministry of National Insurance in those early days built up a reputation for kindness and courtesy, and a disposition to help and explain, and my experience is that these characteristics are still there in the local offices.

In one of the offices I recall visiting in Yorkshire I met a lovely piece of humour, and all of us had a good laugh. The manager of a fairly big office was discussing the number of applicants. One of the difficulties was making out the nature of the illness described on the medical certificate. The manager at random pulled out of the filing cabinet an applicant's form claiming benefit. We just could not make out the nature of the illness. We all had guesses and eventually we all came to the conclusion that it was 'Puerperal Fever'. On looking at the name of the applicant we discovered it was a male person. Legibility is a good thing in saving time!

Not the least important part of the work of the present Ministry of Social Security is dealing with personal calls, with a variety of enquiries. This was envisaged even in the early days of 1945. We were of the opinion that this was a tremendous human job and our endeavour and hope were to translate our ideals into practicalities. I have a pleasant memory which goes back now twenty-five years to the Second Reading of the National Insurance Bill in 1946, after months of painstaking work of discussion. To a crowded House of Commons the Minister, Jim Griffiths, uttered these words which epitomized my own thoughts and feelings: 'For a generation, I have lived with the consequences of insecurity. To those who profess to fear that security will weaken the moral fibre and destroy self-respect, let me say this: it is insecurity that destroys; it is fear of tomorrow that paralyses the will. It is the frustration of human hopes that corrodes the soul. Security will release our people from the haunting fears of yesterday and their gifts to the nation.' My own experience in life and the experience of generations before my time is that insecurity in times of sickness, disability and old age has hung like a millstone round the necks of millions of people. I have heard too often the cries of millions: 'What shall I do? Where shall I go, if adversity comes?'

In 1946, a start was made on an extensive scale to tackle the problem. It was only a beginning, but it was long overdue for insecurity is a nightmare. However, there is still a long way to go. The insecurity of the late 1920s and the 1930s and long before, was to my generation a part of life and a bitter experience. There was a need for a blow to be struck at this monster of insecurity. Such insecurity and poverty is not so prevalent now but we are not yet at the end of the road. 1946 brought only the laying of secure foundations upon which a structure could be built that would give refuge and security from poverty. There is still much to be done, particularly for the elderly and for those who are lonely, and also for the long-term cases of sickness, the disabled and the mentally and physically handicapped. I applaud and welcome the efforts of those who agitate for greater action on behalf of these people.

After nearly five busy and exciting years the election of 1950 came, after which I became the Parliamentary Secretary. This was a new role and gave me the opportunity of speaking from the despatch box and answering questions. The latter were a mixed bag concerned with matters connected with the Department and arising from the legislation of the previous Parliament. There were debates on pnuemoconiosis, turberculosis among nurses and a Bill to assist the old cases under the Workmen's Compensation Acts. I was fortunate in working with Edith Sumerskill, the Minister. She was a skilled Parliamentarian, having had a hectic time when she was Parliamentary Secretary at the Ministry of Food from 1945, a period during rationing.

The visiting of the local offices scattered throughout the country, continued. Eighteen months was all too short a time but, when the next election came, in 1951, my active association, after six years in all, came to an end.

I derived great pleasure in the knowledge that I was privileged to be in at the beginning of what was a great venture and to have shared in the task of creating the Welfare State.

CHAPTER XIII

Parliamentary Delegations
and visits abroad

There are two organizations connected with Parliament to which the majority of members belong. They are the Commonwealth Parliamentary Association, which has branches in most countries throughout the Commonwealth, and the Inter-Parliamentary Union which has branches in most countries throughout the world. The purpose of both is for members of Parliament to maintain contact with Parliaments wherever there is a branch and to arrange visits inward and outward. This is an admirable arrangement for keeping contact and seeing at first-hand the work of government and the conditions, economic and social, in various countries. Each nation has something to learn from another. The social contacts too are productive of much good, and personal friendships are formed which are valuable. Additional to these arrangements, the Foreign Office organizes visits to countries abroad, and the Ministry of Defence arranges visits to the Forces at home and overseas. Before the advent of travel by air, the journeys were long, particularly by sea, to such places as Australia and New Zealand. Now delegations take much less time and achieve the same objective.

My first visit abroad was through the Foreign Office, in January 1946, a few months after the end of the war with Germany. It was to Poland. It may have been one of the first Parliamentary delegations after the war to have discussions with Poland's government. Certainly it was the first from the British Parliament. There were eight in the delegation: four Labour members, three Tories and one Communist. Every member of the delegation knew what Poland had suffered and

165

what losses, human and physical, she had sustained. To describe it adequately is not possible; it had to be seen to be believed. Poland had been liberated from the German occupation only a few months before, and the scars were still there.

On our arrival in Warsaw, we were taken round the city. It was not a matter of what had been destroyed or damaged, but what had escaped. The destruction of property was colossal. Whole areas had been razed to the ground. The first task in reclamation and repair, it seemed to me, was for the authorities to determine where and how to make a beginning. We saw much of the country economically and socially. After twenty-five years, memories of what I saw and heard still linger. Not to have been impressed and emotionally moved was impossible unless you had a heart of stone. We were informed by the government that destruction of materials such as transport and machinery amounted to sixty per cent of Poland's pre-war possessions. Economically the country was operating in a very low gear. The poor state of communications was all too obvious; indeed there was no railway system left in Warsaw. Part of our itinerary was to visit Silesia, in the southern part of the country. This was a thousand miles from Warsaw. There were no trains so the journey was made by car. Travelling along, we could still see evidence of the war: destroyed bridges, damaged guns and burnt-out tanks by the score on the roadside. It was a journey across the European plain I shall long remember, not for the countryside as such but for the effects of the war.

In Silesia we visited factories and steel works and went down one of the coal-mines. All the workers were aware not only of what they had endured during the war, but of the task that lay ahead in restoring the economy of the country. We met members of the government and people belonging to all political parties. We discussed with them their internal problems which, as will be seen, were not only numerous but acute. We were well received wherever we went and we noticed how quickly the people were getting down to their Herculean task of bringing order out of chaos. Their hopes and optimism were high as was their spirit and enthusiasm.

In 1939 Poland had a population of twenty-eight million;

in 1945 it was twenty-five per cent less. Seven million were either killed in combat or died in concentration camps. The delegation had the unforgettable experience of visiting the Auschwitz Camp. It was in a remote place, a Polish village called Oswiecim. It seemed to me as remote as Dartmoor. We were conducted round the camp by a Polish lawyer who was to conduct Poland's case at the Nuremburg Trials. The camp was intact except for the gas chambers which had been destroyed by the retreating Germans as the Russian army advanced. We were told by the guide that five million people, the majority of whom were Jewish, had lost their lives at this camp and, at one time, bodies were being burnt at the rate of 20,000 a day. The Prime Minister, Mr Cyrankiewicz, with whom we had many conversations, had been a prisoner here for five years. He made little reference to his experience; our information came from the guide, whose account was so lurid that it was a sickening and disturbing experience to hear it. It is beyond imagination that men and women could sink into such depths of degradation as was related to us and later revealed at Nuremburg. As I stood there that wintry, snowy afternoon, I expressed my thought to my friend, Dr Stephen Taylor, one of the delegation, that only time could be the healer between the Polish people and the Germans. The scars from the wounds inflicted would remain a long time.

I would still like to see Poland again and witness at first hand the progress of a quarter of a century in every sphere of Polish life.

My next visit abroad was to Finland, seven years later, in 1953—eight years after the end of the war. Finland had not been so involved. There appeared no sign of physical damage and Helsinki the capital, compared with Warsaw, was paradise.

The forests which we visited were a pleasant sight but they are more than that to the Finns. They referred to them as the 'green gold' of Finland because they were such an important part of their economic life. We discovered that there were six political parties represented in Parliament, and that their members of Parliament are elected by proportional representation, with elections every three years.

In connection with industry, we visited a paper mill. The

journey, by rail, to the mill, situated 120 miles north of Helsinki, afforded great pleasure. We passed lakes which, like the forests, are a pleasant feature of Finland. In the continuous stretches of forest, there were spruce pine and silver birch trees for as far as the eye could see. During a conversation with the manager of the paper mill, I was intrigued to hear that he was proudly referring to the usefulness of Finland's rivers and lakes not only as a means of transport but as a pleasure in summer for people could jump straight out of the sauna bath into the lake. A sauna is more than a bath in Finland; it is an institution. No family is without its sauna bath which is attached to the house. The manager pointed out his house which was on the other side of the lake from the mill, a distance of two or three miles, but by road fifteen. 'I find the lake useful in winter time,' he said; 'I go by car across for the ice is three feet thick and so is very reliable and safe.'

I returned from Finland with great affection for the Finns and their country.

Often the remark is made that it is a small world. I thought so at a reception given by the British Finnish Society in Helsinki. I was introduced to the Anglican vicar, the Reverend Isherwood. His parish was extensive for he had clerical responsibility for the Anglican church in Finland and Moscow. The previous day he had just returned from Moscow. When I said I was from Nottinghamshire he told me that he had been in Beeston as Vicar at one time, and that his wife came from Stonebroom, a small mining village in Derbyshire, only ten miles from my home.

In 1954 the Iraq Petroleum Company, which had oil concessions in the Middle East, invited a delegation from the Fuel and Power group of the Labour and Tory parties in the House of Commons to visit Iraq. This was accepted by both groups, and with Harold Neal from the Derbyshire coal-field and Joe Slater from the Durham coal-field, I was chosen to be one of the delegation. The delegation was invited to the headquarters in London a few days before departure to be informed of the places on the proposed itinerary and the extensive operations in oil production. There was a funny coincidence (at least I thought so) at this informal meeting. Dr

Barber, the public relations' officer of the Company said to me, 'The managing director of the Company is here to welcome you. He is a Nottinghamshire man from a place near to Mansfield and expressed a wish to meet you.' After the introduction, we chatted, during the course of which he told me his parents lived at Rempstone in South Nottinghamshire near to the Leicestershire border. 'Ah,' said I, 'that rings a bell. Do your parents live at Manor House? Does your father grow sage, and is his name George Gibson, a member of Basford Rural District? Has he a life-long friend by the name of Matt. Holland of Selston who is a cousin of your father?' 'That is so,' he replied, 'and my name is Stephen Gibson.' 'Well,' I said, 'what a coincidence! Further, Matt. Holland's aunt married my uncle and he is a cousin of your father. We shall soon have family relationships!' It was only a few months before that I had visited his father with Matt. Holland. We agreed it was a small world!

The day of departure arrived. Travelling by air, we came down at Tripoli in the Lebanon where we spent the night. Tripoli was important as it was one of the oil terminals on the Mediterranean coast. The oil was piped across the Syrian desert, hundreds of miles from Iraq to this coastal city of Tripoli, then pumped into sea-going tankers for shipment to Britain and other countries. The oil could be called 'the black gold of the Middle East'. Its importance was apparent, and was challenging the traditional fuel of coal.

Even after a few hours in Tripoli, we could feel the tension and appreciate the dangers of the Middle East. From there we journeyed by air to Kirkuk, a growing and thriving town in Iraq. Its new-found prosperity was based on oil wells which were scattered all over the place, producing huge quantities of oil. During our stay in Kirkuk, an ancient town with a history, we made one interesting visit to the everlasting fires, a piece of waste ground, where, through the seepage of oil, there is a constant flame. The Iraquis believe it to be the scene of the burning fiery furnace into which the three Jews, Shadrack, Meshak and Abednigo were thrown on the instructions of Nebucadnezzar. There is also a legend that to walk through them will guarantee fertility. I said to John Eden, M.P., 'Come on, John. You're a bachelor, no doubt with prospects. You had better walk through them to avoid future disappointment. To me it is of no consequence but I would not like you to be disappointed.'

The delegation travelled thousands of miles from Mosul in the north to the Trucial States at the southern end of the Persian Gulf, visiting oil wells in commission, sites of drilling operations, refineries and terminals on the coast from which places the oil was shipped, passing over thousands of square miles of arid desert.

Three of us were coal-miners, representing mining constituencies and we had sombre thoughts as to the effect this new-found fuel, in such quantity, was likely to have on the coal industry in Britain. The oil revenues of these countries were big and some of this revenue was being used on social projects. At Sumarra in Iraq we witnessed a project to prevent the flooding of Baghdad. At a place called Waddi Thartha a huge dam had been built to conserve the water supply. The opening of this by the young King took place during our visit, and we attended the ceremony. We saw hospitals, schools and houses either completed or in construction. This new-found treasure, the Klondyke of Arabia, was awakening to social consciousness and rightly so.

For centuries this was a pastoral area with its nomads travelling by camel, subsisting on primitive agricultural methods of production. Now the geologists with their knowledge of the earth's resources and their seismic instruments, the engineers and the technicians with their modern equipment constantly discovering and using nature's resources, have brought great changes in the economic, social and political climate of the Middle Eastern countries. The plod of the camel along the trade routes of the desert has been replaced by the noise of drilling going deep into the desert and bringing change in the habits and lives of the people. I recall an incident on a new housing estate: we were invited by an Arab family into their home. The wife and mother of the household was not wearing the traditional veils, to the surprise of those who knew about Arab customs. When she consented to be photographed without the veil and in the company of men who were strangers, the photographers remarked that they had never known this to happen before. As customs and traditions recede into the past, the shy, secluded Arab woman may find a new freedom.

The political problems of the Arab world were much in the minds of the people, overshadowing everything else. The problems could not be swept under the carpet and no one could pretend a tense and volatile situation did not exist. I do not claim to know the answers to their problems. What I was sure about at the time was that, in the parts of the Middle East I was privileged to see, a process of change had begun. It was a visit full of interest, and for the opportunity of seeing so many places overflowing with history I was, and still am, grateful.

In 1957 I was one of a delegation from the Commonwealth Parliamentary Association to visit Tanganyika. Until the end of the First World War in 1918 it was a German colony, known as German East Africa. In June 1919 it was part of the peace treaty that Germany renounced all her rights over her overseas possessions which included German East Africa. It was agreed by the principal allied and associated powers that Britain should assume responsibility for this colony. In 1946, the mandate was transferred to the trusteeship of the United Nations Charter, and continued to be administered by Britain under the auspices of the Colonial Office for the United Nations. So this arrangement continued until she became an independent sovereign state, now known as Tanzania.

Territorially it is a big country but only a part of the larger African continent. At the time of my visit there was a population of 8,500,000, made up of 8,250,000 Africans, 100,000 Asians and 30,000 Europeans. Maybe in the last thirteen years the numbers have increased. Tanzania has 370,000 square miles so there is no problem of space for the population. Prior to Independence the type of administration was British. It had a legislature with ministers and other members. The head was the Governor who had wide powers, similar to those of other Governors in British Colonial territories. The Governor at the time of our visit and until Independence was Sir Edward Twyning, who was much loved. There were a number of able men from Britain in the administration acting as non-elected ministers. They were responsible for the services of education, social welfare, communications, mineral exploration and agriculture. This was my first visit to a British Colony and my first preoccupation was to study their legislature and administration. I had a little information from reading, and from conversations with Jim Griffiths who had been Secretary of State for the Colonies. Arthur Skeffington, M.P., one of the delegation, was a helpful colleague, and was more knowledgeable on colonial matters than I. Recently he died and this reference to him is a tribute to a colleague who was so helpful, both before our visit and during the time we were together in Tanganyika. The experience of being there and seeing and hearing things at first hand proved that this was the best tutor. I soon discovered there were problems and difficulties, but it is like this the world over. At whatever stage of development there is always some kind of problem : it is part of the process of the evolution of society.

On the outward journey, we arrived at Khartoum to refuel. It was 3.00 a.m. We alighted from the plane to stretch our legs. It was dark but the heat was terrific. The canteen was like a bakehouse oven. I recall remarking how hot it was and was told it was 93 degrees fahrenheit. During the previous day, the temperature had been 120 degrees. Our stay was short. We did not leave the airport and consequently saw nothing of Khartoum but my thoughts did wander to my history lessons at school and the first of my thoughts were General Gordon, and the second my mother's brother who was in Khartoum as a serving soldier in the 1880s and was permanently afflicted with illness as a consequence.

On arrival in Tanganyika after a night in Nairobi, we were met and welcomed by Ministers and driven to Government House in Dar-es-Salaam, the capital town of the territory. During my short stay in Nairobi, I received a telephone call. The caller said he was from Mansfield and that he had read in the Nairobi press of my visit with the British Parliamentarians. He was the son of George Bestwick with whom I worked at Sherwood Pit. I spent the day with him and two others, close friends of mine who had made a journey of 200 miles from Nunuki. Reg and Ann Lee had been in Kenya a number of years, and to see them again was a pleasure.

The day after we arrived in Dar-es-Salaam, we were given a well-planned itinerary in order to allow us to see as much as possible of the territory. I looked at the time-table and the omission of one thing disappointed me, and I said so: there was no provision to meet the employers and the Trade Union people. I do not think it was a deliberate omission. It had not occurred to those responsible for the arrangement that it would be desired. I intimated my interest in Industrial Relations and said that there were industries and employers I would like to see and meet. My information was that Trade Unions, although of recent birth, existed and I was expecting and hoping I could meet some of their members.

When I returned to London and would be asked by colleagues about the Trade Union Movement and Industrial relations, I did not want to confess that I had met no one. Arrangements were soon made to enable me to do this. I had to forego seeing other things, including a visit to a diamond mine but I regarded the former as more important. I discovered the Trade Union movement was in its infancy. They were Craft Unions, federated under the Tanganyika Federation of Labour. It was not until the early 1950s that the Trade Union movement began to emerge. The Federation was described to me as the equivalent of the British T.U.C. and had not been formed until 1955, only two years before our visit. Numerically it was small. In January 1957, it had a membership of 30,000 and the number of Unions affiliated was fourteen. The number of persons employed in the various industries in the territory was 480,000. There was a big job ahead in the field of recruitment and organization. Mr Kawawa, the secretary of the Federation, impressed me as an able man. I felt he would do well and would have a useful future. I liked him and we became friends. I have pleasant memories of a number of interesting conversations with him. He was a member of the Legislature and, when Independence came, I was not surprised to learn that he had become Vice-President, an able lieutenant to Julius Nyerere, the President.

I met and conversed with others in Dar-es-Salaam and Tanga, giving them all the encouragement I could in words for it was for them a new sphere. I reminded them that the Trade Union movement in Britain had grown and developed from small beginnings. They were delighted to hear from a person from Britain the history, or some of it, of the Trade Union movement. They were not unmindful of their inexperience and were willing to learn. Their enthusiasm compensated for their inexperience and was a tonic to witness. I met employers on the docks, on the sisal estates and in garages, and discussed the problems of industry with them. Most of them were from Britain and were acquainted with industry. After thirteen years, I still have memories of the many people I met in this eastern part of Africa. Among them were Africans born in Tanganyika, Asians and Europeans who had migrated there, all of them making a contribution to the economic, social and political life of the territory.

At the reception at Government House, the delegation met the Governor. He called me on one side and said. 'You were a coal-miner, I understand, and come from a mining area. Tomorrow I am going to open a research station in Dodoma; I want you to come along with me.' I was the only one of the party to be invited. It was a distance of 400 to 500 miles and we were to go by plane. I arrived at Government House the next morning and wasn't I surprised? We left for the airport escorted by outriders. Arriving at the research station in Dodoma, we proceeded to a geological department which had twenty-two geologists prospecting in the territory for minerals. They had to make long journeys by plane to remote places, bringing back pieces of rock for analysis. At the time of my visit there were in the station 70,000 pieces of individual rock of the strata from north, south, east and west of the territory. The geologists were very optimistic about the mineral resources.

During my stay in Tanga, I visited sisal estates. At one of them I was told by the owner that he employed 1,500 men. The next sentence shocked me: 'They are paid sixty shillings per month which includes food and accommodation for a minimum of four hours per day.' I think he was conscious of the shock he had given me, for he said, 'Of course, those who work longer can earn more.' He said, 'Last year [that was 1956] I made £115,000 profit.' It was no surprise to me that the Trade Union organization was taking root.

I was in Tanganyika for a month. I paid visits to hospitals, a veterinary and farm research station and to an area where there was an irrigation scheme to irrigate 1,500 acres of land for growing ground-nuts. I visited a number of schools. In particular I remember a school for the blind. There I was much moved. It was the work of the Church Army organization. In charge was Captain Varley. I admired his courage and patience, and his devotion to the African children who were being taught in Braille. All I saw and heard seemed to me part of a process of preparation for Independence.

I was convinced that the British administrators as trustees for the United Nations, were doing a good job and the seeds that they were sowing in the form of guidance and help would produce a worthwhile harvest. When self-government came, as it should and must, there would be the foundations upon which the Africans could build, and the work that was being done would have the appreciation of the population, particularly the indiginous part. I found the momentum for self-government was increasing. The Africans were enthusiastic about it. Though the majority of them had not had the advantages of education, some had, like Mr Kawawa and Julius Nyerere, the most colourful figure in Tanganyika. I met Julius Nyerere and found him an able and delightful character, fired with a zeal and enthusiasm for the freedom of his people, who certainly had great affection for him. The question of Independence was on the lips and in the minds of the whole population. The question was not would it come, but when would it come. Within a few years, in 1966, 'freedom' or 'Uhuru' as it is called, arrived. I wrote a congratulatory letter to Julius, now the President of Tanzania. He replied and referred to our meeting in 1957. He had not forgotten. I still have his letter.

Before leaving London I was asked by Jim Griffiths to visit, if possible, a compatriot of his, a Dr Williams, who had been in the Colonial Medical Service for forty years. He was retired and living in the mountain area of Mgamba, five miles north of the town of Lushoto. I was able to do this. On arrival, I discovered the doctor had invited the District Commissioner to supper. Talk went on until midnight. Not the least interesting part of the conversation was their hunting exploits. On retiring, I entered the bedroom to find a log fire; in the bed was a hot-water bottle. This I could not understand. I was in the tropics. But at four in the morning, I put on a cardigan as I was feeling so cold, but when I came down for breakfast, the sun was up and it was hot. I went into the garden and plucked an orange from a tree. I expressed my surprise to Dr Williams and his wife—log fire, water bottle, cardigan and 9.00 a.m. and already hot. 'Yes, my boy,' said the doctor. 'It is like this in these mountains, cool soon after sundown, very hot after the sun is up. Knowing this we made the warm provisions for your comfort.' The day I was leaving for home, I called on the Governor to pay my respects and express my gratitude for the opportunity afforded me in meeting so many people and seeing so much of the Territory and its institutions. He was generous in his appreciation of the delegation's work and interest. Then came a great surprise. 'Look!' he said. 'I would like you to stay here for twelve months.' 'You must be joking!' I said. 'Well', said the Governor, 'I have heard of your meetings with the Trade Union people and the employers, and I recall your speech at the farewell dinner. Also I have heard of your interest in Industrial Relations.' He expressed the opinion that I would be useful in an advisory capacity. I told him, respectfully, that I had neither the desire nor intention of staying in the tropics at sixty-two years of age. Also I could not neglect my Parliamentary duties and my constituency for such a long time. He then asked if I would see Sir Vincent Tewson, at this time Secretary of the British Trade Union Congress, and ask him to send out people with experience to advise and help. I met Sir Vincent and gave him the Governor's message. Both he and the General Council were much in favour of the idea. The difficulty was that so many of the developing countries were making similar requests and it was not an easy matter to meet all of them. This was the climax to an interesting visit.

With Independence the name was changed to Tanzania, a combination of Tanganyika and Zanzibar, that beautiful off-shore island in the Indian Ocean. It has a new name, but it has the same people, who used to voice 'Uhuru' meaning Independence. It is no longer a colony or a territory but a country in Africa and part of the Commonwealth. It has its own Government responsible for finding its own solutions to its own problems. Julius Nyerere, the Leader and first President, is an able man and a well disposed person; I believe equal to the task. I wish him and the people of Tanzania every success.

My next visit abroad was to Canada, in 1965. It was to be my last visit as a member of the House of Commons. What a gathering it was—truly international in character! Every Parliament in the world, with the exception of China, was represented. Many subjects of world interest were discussed and were of great educational value. One difficulty common to all international gatherings is language. Normally the procedure takes a lot of time. You hear the speaker, followed by the interpreter. Canada uses a time-saving system. Instead of benches as at Westminster, there are desks at which each member sits—his own desk too! There are headphones on each desk and whatever language is being spoken, is interpreted into a number of languages and, to hear the one you wish, you just press the appropriate button. Although you are looking at a speaker talking in what is to you a foreign language, it comes to your ears as English. This system was an innovation for the Conference but it is common practice in the Canadian Parliament. It is a bilingual Parliament, English- and French-speaking. It is an excellent piece of organization and must ensure a great economy in time.

The Canadians were wonderful hosts and their welcome and hospitality were very lavish.

The Canadian Government was in the midst of making preparations to celebrate one hundred years of self-government. The year was 1965 and in two years they would be celebrating the centenary of Independence. They were very proud of their achievements in a hundred years and they were justified in their pride.

What a big country Canada is! I did not realize the immensity until I had been there. So much of it is still unexplored. A mention of its territorial vastness reminds me of the story of a lady in London. She had two sons, one of whom had emigrated and was living in Vancouver, while the other remained in London. She decided to visit her son in Vancouver. Everything had been organized including the flight. The son in London wrote to his brother, giving the travel details and expressed the hope he would meet their mother at Montreal airport. The brother replied to the one in London that *he* should meet the mother as he would be the nearest! Montreal is nearer to London than Vancouver which is in the extreme west of Canada.

The year of the exhibition Expo 1967 came, and the British branch of the Commonwealth Parliamentary Association were invited to send a delegation. I was now a member of the House of Lords and, with Lord Drumalbin and others from the House of Commons, I went to see Expo 67. The exhibition was a masterpiece of planning and organization. From every country there were pavilions; it was truly international. It was wonderful and the Government of Canada did the operation well. Apart from a visit to the Upper Canada Village and Niagara with Senator Grosart as our guide, the whole time was spent at the exhibition. However, we met not only Canadians but people from all over the world who had come to see Canada from early primitive time to the present day. This visit, along with the others, was a great experience, and I shall always cherish what my eyes beheld, and the people with whom I had conversations.

CHAPTER XIV

House of Lords

If I had been told when I began to be active in my political life, and even before then—for instance behind the door in the pit as a door trapper, that one day I should be a member not only of the House of Commons but later of the House of Lords too, I would have dismissed the idea as rubbish. I might even have suggested that whoever said it had taken leave of his senses and allowed his imagination to run riot. It would have been something more than even a miracle for it was not even in my thinking.

Sixty years ago, indeed even less, there were only a few working men from the pits, the factories and the manual occupations, who were ever members of the House of Commons. A limited franchise and personal economic circumstances made it almost impossible. It was not until 1911 that payment of members of the House of Commons was established making it easier for working men and people with limited financial resources to stand as candidates for election to the House of Commons. To become a member of the House of Lords, the bastion of the hereditary principle, confined exclusively to men with hereditary titles of the first creation, or successors to titles, some of them going back for centuries, was almost impossible before the Life Peerages' Act of 1958. It is no small wonder then, that to people like myself, it was not in our thinking, even if the desire was there. It was a 'closed shop', almost confined to those who had succeeded to the titles of their forebears.

In November 1965, I publically announced my retirement. The election of 1966 came sooner than I thought. The 1964 Parliament lasted only eighteen months. However, whenever the election came, it was to be my last Parliament as a member of the House of Commons. Of course, prior to accommodating myself to retirement, I took part in the election in Mansfield. I also went to Carlisle where Ron. Lewis was seeking re-election as the Labour candidate. Both Dennis Concannon, my successor in Mansfield, and Ron. Lewis were successful. The party too did well, substantially improving its majority as compared with the election of 1964.

A few months before, I had arranged with Michael Foot, M.P., to be my guest and principal speaker at the May Day Meeting in Mansfield. This provided us with an opportunity for reminiscing. The following morning I took him by car to Nottingham to catch an early train. On the station I said, 'When I shall see you again, Michael, is anybody's guess. As I have now retired, the opportunity will be remote, and I bade him goodbye. I returned home. My wife was attending a County Council meeting so, with all the time in the world, I prepared lunch for myself, after which I settled down. How ignorant I was of what was awaiting me! The telephone rang. I still remember the dialogue that took place, and often laugh about it. The first words of the caller were, 'Is that Mr Bernard Taylor, the ex-M.P. for Mansfield?' 'It is,' said I. 'Fine', said the caller. 'This is 10 Downing Street.' 'I know the place', I said. 'The present occupant, the Prime Minister, I also know.' 'That is right', said the caller. Who it was I had no idea and I am still ignorant. He then said, 'Could you come here as soon as possible? The Prime Minister would like to see you and have a talk with you.' There was no indication as to what it was about. The next move was with me. 'What do you mean "As soon as possible"?' I said. 'Oh, could you come today? It is urgent and important.' 'It is now 2.00 p.m. It is too late today,' I said, 'but I could be in London by 10.00 a.m. tomorrow.' 'Fine', said the caller, 'I will arrange the meeting for twelve noon.' This was 3 May 1966. I could only speculate why the Prime Minister wanted to see me.

When I approached the policeman at the door of Number Ten and told him my name I was admitted with no further enquiries. It was not the Cabinet Room into which I was directed. However, the Prime Minister appeared, and no one else was present. The usual pleasantries over, the Prime Minister said, 'Well, Bernard, I am sure you will be wondering why I have asked you to come.' 'Well, I am curious, but I don't for a moment suppose you have asked me to do a journey of three hundred miles and pay my own train fare just to ask me how I am.' 'No,' said the Prime Minister, 'I could have done that by writing, but I have an offer to make.' 'Ah, not the Chairmanship of the National Coal Board,' said I jokingly. 'No', said the Prime Minister. 'There is no vacancy, but I would like you to go to the House of Lords with a Life Peerage.' I was a little surprised and startled. 'Any special reason?' I enquired. 'Yes', was the Prime Minister's answer. He said that the majority of those who were miners in the House of Lords had passed on, and he mentioned George Hall, Gordon McDonald and Jack Lawson. Tom Williams was ill and unlikely to return, leaving Bill Blyton as the only miner. 'There have always been problems in the mining industry', he said, 'and still are, if of a different kind; and there are likely to be whilst there is a mining industry. Further, there will be legislation in the social services field, about which you have some knowledge and experience. Also you have been a Minister and I think you deserve the offer.' The reasons given convinced me I should accept, which I did before I left. I was unable to say anything about my acceptance until the public announcement which was to be three weeks later.

I left Number Ten and, standing at the entrance to Downing Street, I hesitated, wondering what to do next. It was Budget Day in the House of Commons. Should I turn right and hear the speech of the Chancellor of the Exchequer or turn left and make my way to the station for the train home? It occurred to me if I went to the House of Commons, someone would ask, 'What brings you here so soon after retiring? Come to hear the Budget?' In view of what had transpired earlier in the day, and having to keep a secret until the public announcement, I turned to the left and caught the first train for home.

The day the news broke, I was inundated with congratulatory messages and good wishes. A few days after the announcement, I was invited by Garter King of Arms to meet him to discuss the choice of a title and the date of my introduction into the House of Lords. This is the customary practice. The meeting to me was a novel one but pleasant. He was very helpful. The title I thought of and would have preferred was 'Medenwood'. The significance of this is that there is a stream called the River Meden, passing through a vale by the name of Littlewood. It is only one mile from my present home and at no time in my life has been more than two miles away. The stream is the dividing line for the counties of Nottinghamshire and Derbyshire. The Vale of Littlewood is a quiet spot off the beaten track accessible only by foot. I have walked to it hundreds of times. I played there as a boy and fished for tiddlers in the stream with not too elegant gear. As I grew into manhood this vale still had its attractions and I always found quiet and inspiration there in the solitude when ideas and thoughts came to me which I wrote down or said aloud to the stream and the trees. Such may appear to be silly but I personally enjoyed it.

So 'Medenwood' because of these memories appealed to me. and I was attracted to it as a title. However, Mr Christmas, the Town Clerk of Mansfield, suggested it would be fitting and appropriate to identify with the title 'Mansfield' and the constituency which I had represented in the House of Commons for twenty-five years. I thought the suggestion right and proper and changed my thinking about it. I agreed with Garter King of Arms on the title 'Lord Taylor of Mansfield'. There are now three Lord Taylors in the House of Lords. The two others are Lord Taylor of Barnet and Lord Taylor of Gryffe. There are occasions when it is confusing and there are moments when I wish I had chosen 'Medenwood'.

These initial preliminaries over, I was introduced into the House of Lords in June 1966. It was a quiet occasion, with the usual ritual of the wearing of robes and having two sponsors of one's own choosing. My sponsors were Dr Edith Summerskill, now a Baroness, with whom I had worked as Parliamentary Secretary when she was Minister of National Insurance, and Bill Blyton, an old friend and colleague in the House of Commons. He had been made a Life Peer twelve months before my introduction. Like myself, he was a coalminer. We had so much in common and our experience in the Miners' Trade Union Movement was identical although we had spent the whole of our lives in different areas of the coal-fields, he in Durham, myself in Nottinghamshire. There is always an affinity between miners wherever you come from and for both of us it also meant a continuation of active friendship which had begun in the House of Commons more than twenty years before.

In the gallery were my wife, now Lady Taylor, my son, the Hon. Bernard Taylor and his wife, and to these three I am grateful for their help and affection over many years. They have been wonderful. Their forbearance, kindness, and affection I shall always treasure. My grandson, Martin, six and a half years old, was also there. What he thought about it all I do not know. He was certainly curious, and asked questions afterwards about the place and the people. With the passing of time, he often makes a reference to that day in the House of Lords. A few friends were also present: Frank and Eileen Cook of Selston and my successor in the House of Commons, Dennis Concannon.

A few days after my introduction, there was a Bill on Social Insurance matters and upon this I made my maiden speech. It is like the House of Commons: when you have broken the ice by speaking for the first time, you feel part of the place.

If you want to take part in a debate in the Lords the procedure is very different from that in the House of Commons. In the latter, after your maiden speech which is arranged with the Speaker by the Whips, you take your chance—catching the Speaker's eye as it is commonly referred to. It is possible to sit through a whole day's sitting and at the end, after attempting to be called, you have drawn a blank—a frustrating experience. Often members say, and I have thought this myself, 'The best speech of the day is undelivered in your mind or pocket or both, instead of Hansard the official record.' In the Lords a list is prepared of those who wish to speak on the day of the debate. The list of speakers is placed in the Prince's Chamber, and you know when it is your turn. You are not called, as in the Commons. When the Lord previous to you sits down, it is the turn of the next on the list. You rise to address the House by saying 'My Lords' and you continue with your speech. This pattern continues until the list is exhausted. Of one thing you are certain, you make your speech.

The atmosphere in the Lords is different from that in the Commons. The occasions are few when the temperature rises but it does happen. There are occasions when sharp divisions arise on subjects of great controversy, such as divorce, homosexuality, abortion, matters in the social sphere, Rhodesia, apartheid, the Industrial Relations and Immigration Bill, and the Common Market. These are a few of the matters that have been debated during my short period in the House of Lords, all highly controversial matters and of great public concern.

During the last decade since the Life Peerages Act of 1958, the composition of the House of Lords has undergone changes. Before it was composed of hereditary peers. Now there are men and women from every walk of life in the Lords: the professions, the academic world, the Trade Unions and industry. They are people with great experience in their respective spheres. They have recognized ability and specialized knowledge on every subject you can think of. This ensures a high standard of debating skill.

My own experience is short in the Lords, and I am learning as I go along, but I enjoy this new sphere of activity. Occasionally, I sit on committees dealing with Private Bills. I find this absorbingly interesting. Looking back to 1966 I think I would have been mistaken not to have accepted the offer. I have been given the opportunity of taking part in debates and, I say this with modesty, of putting forward views that may not have been ventilated on matters connected with mining and in the social field.

With other colleagues on the highly controversial and hotly contested Industrial Relations' Bill, my experience in the Trade Union movement was an asset, certainly to me. The Labour Peers made a gallant fight on this Bill. It was a prolonged struggle from the time the Bill came from the Commons at the end of March 1971. It was the end of July 1971 before all its stages had been completed. In most weeks between March and July, the Bill was debated for three days. It was a marathon. I doubt whether it would have taken half as long had it not been for the magnificent efforts mainly of the Life Peers. I am certain the opponents of the Bill, of whom I was one, and I felt strongly against it, won the argument, but, as expected, when divisions were called, the opposition lost the votes.

I have made new friends, always a pleasing experience, many of whom I would not otherwise have met. I have no doubt that the House of Lords is a changed and changing place and, in my view, this is due to the creation of so many Life Peers during the past decade : men and women of the calibre I have mentioned. My observations lead me to the view that the influence of the Hereditary Peers, with exceptions on both sides of the Lords, is receding.

CHAPTER XV

Eventide

Although inevitable, eventide can be a useful part of life. It is like morning and afternoon, a part of the day. Activities are fewer; there are not so many calls on your time, and responsibilities diminish. On the other hand, there are opportunities for meditation when you can think of the past, the present and the future. Today and tomorrow reflect the activities of yesterday. This is as true of nations as of individuals. Thinking of the past in isolation, and writing of the way you have travelled, to divorce yourself from the present with its many problems, and turn a blind eye to the potentialities of the future, is a mistake; for what you have done, or even attempted to do, is part only of a collective effort to make today and tomorrow better than yesterday. To endeavour with others to make our world a better place and to strive to bring happiness and security to people has its compensations. I think it was Wordsworth who wrote in one of his poems: 'No endeavour is in vain; its reward is in the doing.' The individual contribution may be small, a drop in the ocean, but it is important, adding to the total effort by thousands of other like-minded folk, desirous and determined to move forward to a better world. There are memories, the more pleasant ones refreshing, and you can see your mistakes which were not deliberate—and who has not made any? Often it has been said, 'He who makes no mistakes, never attempted anything.' Maybe the mistakes were errors of judgement at the time, but 'nothing ventured, nothing achieved'. At eventide you see every milestone: the moments of triumph, and the circumstances of disappointment and frustration. But why should a man be deterred? The mixture of triumph and disappointment is part of man's evolution to a better and more satisfying life.

Many old friends, including some with whom I went to school more than sixty years ago, have made the suggestion that I put on paper some of the reminiscences of 'Life's Journey'. They have said, 'You have seen so much and met so many people. You have taken part in public life over so many years. To have a record would be interesting.' I can only hope they are right.

The Mansfield Parliamentary constituency, its people, and particularly Mansfield Woodhouse, have meant to me much more than I can adequately describe. I find it surprising in moments of meditation, how events and people of years ago emerge from the subconscious mind, clearer than something that happened only yesterday, and memories are revived as fresh and fragrant as the mountain stream.

In an earlier chapter when referring to Mr Stirland, the under-manager at Sherwood pit, I said I would relate an experience. It was one of the happenings I was unable to understand at the time. I think I do now. One day in 1942 or 1943, a man whom I knew called on me. I had not seen him for a number of years. The purpose of his visit was to deliver a message from Mr Stirland, now in failing health, and in the eventide of his life. He had been retired from the pit for twelve years and was living in West Bridgford, near Nottingham. Fifteen years had gone by since I last saw him and I had every reason to think he had forgotten me. I was curious and mystified. I said to the messenger, 'If you are not pulling my leg, of course I will call on him.' I was convinced of the validity of the request. The arrangement was made and I met him at his home. His daughter, whom I had taught in the Sunday School, greeted me at the door and said, 'Father is expecting you and looking forward to seeing you.' In the privacy of his home, for two hours, we talked about a variety of things: politics and parliament and sport, particularly cricket—his house was near the famous Trent Bridge cricket ground. Sherwood pit and the episode in his office were not mentioned. A few months later, he died. During the journey home, I was still mystified as to why he had wanted me to visit him. Rightly or wrongly, I concluded that it was his way, without saying so in so many words, of making his peace with me : let the past be forgotten; let it be buried. With me, and I am sure with him, there were neither hard feelings nor bitterness. Time is a great healer. I was pleased I had responded to his invitation. Possibly it meant much to him; it certainly did to me. He was so profuse in congratulating me on becoming a Member of Parliament, and assuring me of his good wishes in this field of public service for many years to come. Journeying home then, and since, I have whispered to myself the little couplet: 'I know not what the future hath of marvel or surprise' and this episode certainly was a surprise.

Sixty-three years have now passed since I began work at the pit, almost fifty-six years since I entered public life. During this time, which has been of absorbing interest, and has included some exciting days, my activities have assumed different forms: the Sunday School and Chapel, the Trade Union, local government, the House of Commons and the House of Lords. Not one bit of it do I regret. All of it has been interesting and informative and from it all I have cherished memories and experiences. I regard myself fortunate to have been privileged to have had so many opportunities and experiences. When I look back to the beginning of my public life in the village chapel, it does not seem long. It is like the ship that passes in the night, but there have been changes, as there will be in the future. Maybe they will come more quickly. History is full of evidence that man's evolutionary chariot is always on the move, at times with greater momentum and greater speed than at other times. The technological forces that have been released, and the growing economic and social forces will mean continued change in the pattern of society. I learned very early that the only constant thing in the world is change. We must expect it, and bend our effort to ensure what is believed collectively to be the right kind of change.

From the beginning of hitching my waggon to a star, my main interest has been centred on the abolition of poverty and insecurity, twin causes of so much unhappiness, not only in the home but throughout the world. Taking a universal view, I believe there is still a long way to go. Security and peace are the things everybody desires. The words of Blake are as appealing to me today as they were when I sang them either in the chapel or at the Labour meetings: 'I will not cease from mental strife, nor shall my sword sleep in my hand.' With like-minded people, we can build Jerusalem in Britain's green and pleasant land. Not only is there still much to be done here, but also throughout the world which is now only a parish, and must become a neighbourhood where Peace, Plenty and Security reign.

Appendix

Very many years after the events described in Chapter 6 on the Spencer Union, I had the opportunity of seeing the records of the Coal Owners' Deputation Book, which went back to the beginning of the colliery in 1903.
There I found the Owners' minutes of the two deputations led by Mr Spencer and Mr Cooper in the thirties. I think these are of historical interest, and reproduce them here.

30 April 1930

Deputation re Industrial Union
For Industrial Union, Messrs G. A. Spencer, R. Gascoigne
For Sherwood Colliery Co., Messrs L. A. and C. H. Heathcote
Geo. A. Spencer Said that he had come to ask the management to assist to increase the membership of the Industrial Union. At Sherwood Colliery the membership had fallen from 450 to 250. The Notts. Miners Association was growing in the district. Some Companies were willing to deduct the subscription, now 6d per week, where the men had signed an agreement to this effect.
C. H. Heathcote Said it was a very difficult matter to interfere. It had always been the practice at Sherwood Colliery not to influence the men in any way in regard to joining or not joining a union. He asked what other pits did in this matter.
Geo. A. Spencer In most cases the Undermanager assists particularly in the letting of the stalls.
C. H. Heathcote Said the Directors preferred not to interfere and suggested that it would be better to approach the Owners with regard to this question.

Geo. A. Spencer Said that if the Managers and the Under-managers were allowed a little latitude to use their influence, this would be all required to get the men into the Industrial Union. He was trying to arrange a meeting with the owners.

C. H. Heathcote Agreed that the best thing to do was to approach the Owners on this question.

Taken from the Sherwood Colliery's deputation book.

7 June 1934

Deputation for the Notts. and District Miners Industrial Union

Representing the Union :

> Messrs H. Cooper (General Secretary)
> S. Wilcockson (Branch Secretary)
> H. Wheatman (Branch President)
> A. Playfoot (Branch Committee)

Mr Cooper Said the deputation had come to see what they could do in order to increase the membership at Sherwood Colliery. The number of members in the Sherwood branch had fallen seriously since the T.U.C. meeting with the Coal Owners in Nottingham in 1928. The income of the Branch had fallen from £367 for the year 1924 to £162 10s. od. for 1933. The income was still falling and the Branch was having difficulty in carrying on. Taken as a whole the Industrial Union was increasing in numbers and the decrease at Sherwood Colliery was quite exceptional. It was strange that Sherwood Colliery should be the only pit in the district to be losing ground. Would the Company consider deducting from the men's wages a weekly contribution of 6d.

C. H. Heathcote Said the question of the Company deducting the contributions had already been considered by the Board of Directors who refused to do it just as they refused the same request by the old Miners Union. The Company did not like interfering with the liberty of the workmen.

Mr H. Cooper Suggested that the Manager should give preference to members of the Industrial Union when allocating the stalls.

C. H. Heathcote Said that he could hardly expect the Manager to build up the Union.

Mr H. Cooper Some Managers do it in their own way.

Mr C. H. Heathcote Said he did not care to interfere in any way. He would most strongly object to being forced to join any particular body. The Union should stand on its own feet. The real trouble was that the workmen were tired of Unions and realized that if they could obtain fair play they did not require a Union.

Mr H. Cooper Said he was pleased to have been to the Colliery and he hoped that G.H.N. would be able to help them.

22 November 1935

Deputation of workmen employed in the 'Dunsil seam'. The coal getters did not attend work on Nov. 22nd. During the morning Mr B. Taylor rang up Mr C. N. Heathcote, and asked him to meet a deputation of the workmen. He stated that the men were dissatisfied with their wages. Mr C. N. Heathcote agreed to meet a deputation of the workmen but refused to meet either Mr Taylor or Mr Coleman.

Mr C. H. Heathcote Said he was unable to meet Mr Taylor or Mr Coleman as the owners had given an undertaking to Mr Spencer that they would not acknowledge any Union but the Industrial Union.

12 June 1936

Deputation of the Industrial Union

Mr Geo. A. Spencer. Wished to raise two matters, *viz*

(1) The small membership of the Sherwood Colliery Branch of the Union.

(2) The rate of wages paid to face workers, and the conditions under which they had to work.

The first matter was old standing and he could only ask the Manager and Undermanager to help in building up the numbers.

Mr L. A. Heathcote Said he was prepared to help the Union in any legitimate way, but the building up of the Union was the job of the Union officials not of the Colliery officials. In regard to wages and conditions at the face the position was improving and was expected to improve as the faces got away from the break at the peak of the anti-cline. Could Mr Spencer suggest any method by which the Manager and Undermanager could assist the Union?

Mr Geo. Spencer If the Union could negotiate a price list it would help the Union.

C. A. Heathcote Suggested that the Union should bring a deputation of 'Dunsil' men to fix a list for that seam.

Mr Geo. Spencer If Mr Heathcote could get six or seven of the Dunsil seam men to join the Industrial Union it would be possible to arrange a list.

Mr C. A. Heathcote The Company would be prepared to negotiate immediately for a list if the Union could bring a deputation of the 'Dunsil' workmen.

Mr Geo. Spencer Suggested that members of the Industrial Union should have preference when stalls are being let. He also suggested that separate contracts should be arranged in the conveyor stalls.

Mr C. A. Heathcote Would not agree with this.

Mr Geo. Spencer Said he hoped Mr C. A. Heathcote (Manager) and Mr R. Stubbs (Undermanager) would do all they could for the Industrial Union. They had the influence if they would use it. The deputation would leave it at that.

For the Industrial Union
> Messrs Geo. A. Spencer
> S. Wilcockson
> A. Playfoor
> H. Wheatman

For the Colliery Company
> Mr C. A. Heathcote (Manager)
> Mr N. Stubbs (Undermanager)

Afterword

by Rt Hon. James Griffiths, C.H.

Uphill All the Way is a deeply moving story, told with fidelity and modesty, of one man's struggles, disappointments and achievements. It was worth the telling as a human story. It has the added value of being a faithful chronicle of a crucial period in the history of British coal miners and their trade union. The reader has gained fuller understanding of the 'grass roots' of the Trade Union and Labour Movement.

Here we found a vivid portrait of a working-class home at the turn of the century; the parents for whom life was one long struggle to make both ends meet, and where the coming of the fourth child (the unwanted child) only deepened the poverty of the family. As that fourth child, Bernard had to seek work at eleven years of age, and as he grew up so did the new coal-field as pits were sunk on the fringes of Notts. Forest. It seemed in the fitness of things that as soon as he reached the age of thirteen he should begin his career as a coal miner. As one whose early life followed a similar pattern, I found his portrayal of those first days down the mine full of nostalgic memories. The haunting fears of the 'door-boy' left alone in the dark cavern; the lad who finds courage to face the dangers in the friendship of the pit ponies; the collier lad whose life is enriched by the fellowship of common danger. All these experiences stirred his imagination and led to the awakening to a larger life—and so to the Methodist church where he discovered and developed those gifts which were later to be used in the service of his trade union, the Labour

194

party and parliament. Bernard's story confirms the truth of the saying that the British Socialist movement owes more to Methodism than to Marx.

His public career began at a time when, after a century of continuous expansion, the coal mining industry was beginning to contract. The 1914-1918 war had virtually destroyed the coal export trade with ruinous results for the older coal-fields, and newer coal-fields like Notts. were being affected by the beginnings of the transition to a multiple fuel economy. After 1918 the slide to the 'depression' accelerated, and inevitably led to the strikes of 1921 and 1926. The nine-month struggle of 1926 was a traumatic experience for the miners. They fought until they were exhausted. In the Notts. coal-field one miners' leader broke ranks and, in alliance with the coal owners, organized a return to work and formed a rival union. Coming as it did at a time when the miners felt deserted, and that the whole world was against them, this was a supreme test of character. Bernard was one of the stalwarts who remained firm in their allegiance to the old union. The period of dual struggle—of miners against masters, and of the 'Old' against the 'Gaffers' Union (as the men called it) was to continue for many years. It is epitomized in the story of Harworth, faithfully chronicled in *Uphill All the Way*. How strange that this epic struggle should have been waged in a new coal mine, set in an old world village in the countryside which is the setting of D. H. Lawrence's novel *Sons and Lovers*. The struggle begun at Harworth spread into other coal-fields, and meantime the industry continued to slide into the depression of the thirties. I remember exchanging experiences with Bernard during this period, and he said to me, 'The old Book has a verse for all occasions and when pondering over the bitter feeling in the pits, this one comes to mind : "The fathers have eaten sour grapes and the children's teeth are set on edge".'

As thousands of miners were thrown on the road and those at work were impoverished and humiliated by owners and governments, it was natural that young miners' leaders like Bernard should look to politics, and to Labour's plans for public ownership as the only hope of salvation for the miners. Having served his apprenticeship in local government, he eventually found his way to parliament as Member for his native heath.

The Labour Party has succeeded because it is a combination of idealists and pragmatists. The political activities of Bernard Taylor, M.P., as told in these pages reveals the idealist-pragmatist at work.

My friendship with Bernard, which began in the heart-breaking years of conflict in the twenties, continued as we both worked for our party through the vicissitudes of the inter-war years and the trials of the Second World War. Then came the Labour victory of 1945 and the opportunity for our friendship to ripen into a close partnership as we worked together in the Ministry of National Insurance. It was our privilege, with our colleagues, to embody the Beveridge Plan for social security in legislation, and to establish the nationwide organization to administer the new scheme.

Sometimes when I am visited by my old friend, we look back over the years; although not everything has turned out as we had hoped, we console ourselves with the thought that things are better now for the coal miners and the prospect better for our grandchildren, and in spite of the fears that haunt the world and the wars that still plague mankind our faith and our hope remain as we repeat again the words of our favourite hymn:

'These things shall be, a loftier race than ere the world has known shall rise, with flame of Freedom in their souls—and Light of Knowledge in their eyes.'

Index